Data Science and Machine Learning Interview Questions using **Python**

A Complete Question Bank to Crack Your Interview

by
Vishwanathan Narayanan

SECOND REVISED AND UPDATED EDITION 2020
FIRST EDITION 2019
Copyright © BPB Publications, India
ISBN: 978-93-89845-785

All Rights Reserved. No part of this publication may be reproduced or distributed in any form or by any means or stored in a database or retrieval system, without the prior written permission of the publisher with the exception to the program listings which may be entered, stored and executed in a computer system, but they can not be reproduced by the means of publication.

LIMITS OF LIABILITY AND DISCLAIMER OF WARRANTY

The information contained in this book is true to correct and the best of author's & publisher's knowledge. The author has made every effort to ensure the accuracy of these publications, but cannot be held responsible for any loss or damage arising from any information in this book.

All trademarks referred to in the book are acknowledged as properties of their respective owners.

Distributors:

BPB PUBLICATIONS
20, Ansari Road, Darya Ganj
New Delhi-110002
Ph: 23254990/23254991

MICRO MEDIA
Shop No. 5, Mahendra Chambers,
150 DN Rd. Next to Capital Cinema,
V.T. (C.S.T.) Station, MUMBAI-400 001

Ph: 22078296/22078297
DECCAN AGENCIES
4-3-329, Bank Street,
Hyderabad-500195
Ph: 24756967/24756400

BPB BOOK CENTRE
376 Old Lajpat Rai Market,
Delhi-110006
Ph: 23861747

Published by Manish Jain for BPB Publications, 20 Ansari Road, Darya Ganj, New Delhi-110002 and Printed at Repro India Ltd, Mumbai

Dedicated to

Dedicated to Pratyangira, Bala, Durga, Mom, Dad, Chitti my aunt, my sister Ishwarya, Sridhar my brother in law and to all my mentors especially Shiv without whom this book would still be a dream. Also the support extended by Shyam Sir, Khadak and BPB Publications is very much appreciated.

*Durga has been a great inspiration for this book.
She has always been and will me my encouragement to write more books.*

Also remember Sudarshan as a friend in need.

Also dedicated to my students from whom I equally learned as I taught them.

Along with all the blessing of almighty is also remembered here without which even a blade of grass does not move

About the Author

Mr Vishwanathan has twenty years of hard code experience in the software industry spanning across many multinational companies and domains. Playing with data to derive meaningful insights has been his domain and that is what took him towards data science and machine learning.

Preface

Data science is one of the hottest topics mainly because of the application areas it is involved and things which were once upon of time, impossible with earlier software has been made easy. This book tries to comprehend the ocean of data science into small book which is mainly intended to be used as last minute revision. Before interview, all the important concepts have been given in simple and understand format.

This book tries to include various terminologies and logic used both as a part of Data Science and Machine learning for last minute revision. As such you can say that this book acts as a companion whenever you want to go for interview.

Simple to use words have been used in the given answers for the questions to help ease of remembering and representation of same. Examples where ever deemed necessary have been provided so that same can be used while giving answers in interview. Author tried to consolidate whatever he came across, on multiple interviews that he attended and put the same in words so that it becomes easy for the reader of the book to give direction on how the interview would be.

With the number of data science jobs increasing, Author is sure that everyone who wants to pursue this field would like to keep this book as a constant companion. Soon, Author will be coming shortly with a new book on R too, so that it makes a complete data science stack.

Happy reading to all the readers, your feedback is highly appreciated.

Foreword

It is not wrong to say that today's dynamic world is driven totally by statistics. With decision making becoming important in being successful the use of software this task has become common, Thanks to the advancement made with respect to technology. While software application always existed for doing the above task , the volume and ability of software programmes to represent complex equation related to statistics and probability was limited.

Thanks to pandas, numpy, scipy and sklearn modules of Python, the above problem faced has been removed to a great extent and the problem is no more a challenge. With complex mathematical concepts easily convertible to algorithms the life of data scientist and analyst has become quite easy.

This book is mainly intended to help people represent their answer in a sensible way to the interviewer. The answers have been carefully rendered in a way to make things quite simple and yet represent the seriousness and complexity of matter. Since data science is incomplete without mathematics we have also included a part of the book dedicated to statistics.

Python has already taught us that small code does not mean lesser powerful the same concept has been adopted to keep the book a powerful weapon for any one attending interview.

Table of Contents

1. Data Science Basic Questions and Terms 1
- Q1: Explain the steps involved in data science? 1
- Q2: Explain variable and different types of variables? 2
- Q3: Explain Categorical measurement? 3
- Q4: Explain Binary variables? 3
- Q5: Explain Nominal measurement? 3
- Q6: Explain Ordinal variable? 3
- Q7: Explain Continuous variables? 3
- Q8: Explain Discrete variables? 3
- Q9: Is it possible to convert continuous values to discrete and vice versa? 3
- Q10: What are interval variables? 3
- Q11: What are ratio variables? 4
- Q12: What are Univariate and Bivariate variables? 4
- Q13: What is measurement error? 4
- Q14: Explain Validity? 4
- Q15: Explain Reliability? 4
- Q16: What are the different ways to test hypotheses? 4
- Q17: Explain the different types of variation? 5
- Q18: Explain repeated-measures design? 5
- Q19: What is independent design? 5
- Q20: Explain the role of randomization w.r.t variation? 6
- Q21: Explain various summary measures 6
- Q22: Explain alternate hypotheses and null hypotheses. 8
- Q23: What is p value? 8
- Q24: What happens when null hypotheses is rejected? 8
- Q25: Explain directional and non-directional hypotheses. ... 8
- Q26: Explain fit of model? 9
- Q27: What is relation between sample and population? 9

Q28: What is estimation? 9
Q29: Explain deviation score? 9
Q30: Explain variance? 9
Q31: Explain Standard deviation. 10
Q32: Explain standard error. 10
Q33: What is precision? 10
Q34: Explain confidence intervals. 11
Q35: Explain confidence level. 11
Q36: Explain alpha. 11
Q37: Explain Beta. 11
Q38: Explain Accuracy. 11
Q39: Explain Bias. 11
Q40: What is central limit theorem? 11
Q41: Explain Absolute value? 12
Q42: What is degree of freedom? 12
Q43: Explain cluster sampling. 12
Q44: Explain Correlation coefficients? 13
Q45: Explain sample space. 13
Q46: What is non parametric algorithm? 13
Q47: How can learning be classified? 13
Q48: What is classification? 14
Q49: Explain the steps involved in classification. 14
Q50: What is regression? 14
Q51: Explain the similarities and differences between
    Classification and Regression. 15
Q52: Explain various terms encountered during
    classification algorithm. 15
Q53: Explain multi class classification? 15
Q54: Explain multi label classification? 16
Q55: Explain how multi label problem can be solved? 16
Q56: Explain some important metrics with respect to
    testing a model? 17
Q57: What is logistic regression? 18

xiii

Q58: Explain Naïve Bayes..18
Q59: What is Stochastic Gradient Descent? 19
Q60: Explain decision tree algorithm. 19
Q61: What is Gini index? 20
Q62: Is Gini index the only means which can be used in decision tree?...20
Q63: What is Pruning w.r.t. decision tree?....................21
Q64: What is random forest? 21
Q65: Explain the difference between Random forest and decision tree. 21
Q66: What is overfitting and underfitting? 22
Q67: What are the reasons for under fitting occurrences? 22
Q68: Does over fitting get affected by noise? 23
Q69: Explain KNN (K Nearest Neighbour) steps involved, advantage and disadvantage...23
Q70: Explain selection bias. 24
Q71: What does selection bias indicate w.r.t. algorithm?..........24
Q72: What is Bootstrap sample? 24
Q73: What is Resampling? 24
Q74: Explain tail. 25
Q75: Explain the difference between one way test and two way test. 25
Q76: Explain degree of freedom. 25
Q77: What is predictive modeling? 25
Q78: What is time series analysis? 25
Q79: What is deep learning? 25
Q80: What is Convolutional Neural Network? 26
Q81: What are different ways to determine optimal value of clusters?. 26
Q82: What are various distance related functions for similarity measures?..26

2. **Python Programming Questions**..................................27
   Q1: Is Python Object oriented? 27

Q2:	Is Python case sensitive?	27
Q3:	What kind of language is Python?	27
Q4:	What are different versions of Python?	27
Q5:	Explain different implementations of Python?	28
Q6:	Is Python loosely typed?	29
Q7:	How to start a new block in Python?	29
Q8:	How to get data type of a particular variable?	29
Q9:	How many ways can Python program be run?	29
Q10:	Explain the importance of Pylint and Pychecker	29
Q11:	Explain Zen of Python.	29
Q12:	How to print Zen in Python?	30
Q13:	Explain Python data types.	30
Q14:	How can we switch variables in Python?	31
Q15:	What is the use of pass statement in Python?	31
Q16:	Is Python pass by value or pass by reference?	31
Q17:	Does Python supports chained operations?	31
Q18:	Explain ALL and ANY.	32
Q19:	Explain the difference between IS and ==.	32
Q20:	Explain supported collection of data type w.r.t. Python?	32
Q21:	Create a simple number list?	33
Q22:	Can you create nested list?	33
Q23:	Explain CRUD (Create, Update, and Delete) operations from list.	34
Q24:	Explain operations in dictionary.	35
Q25:	Explain operation with tuples.	35
Q26:	Explain del?	36
Q27:	If del can remove variable can it remove tuple variable?	36
Q28:	Delete last element in a list.	36
Q29:	Predict the output of following code.	37
Q30:	What do you mean by list comprehension?	37
Q31:	Explain the preferred way for looping through list?	37
Q32:	Find the reverse of the dictionary?	37

Q33:	How to sort dictionary by value?	38
Q34:	What is the use of shuffle function?	38
Q35:	What is the preferred way to get a value based on key in Python?	38
Q36:	Explain alternate way of merging 2 or more dictionaries without using update method?	38
Q37:	What is the preferred way of fetching last element/second last and so on from a list?	39
Q38:	What is the preferred way for reversing a list?	39
Q39:	Explain various string utility functions in Python.	39
Q40:	How to check whether two strings are equal.	40
Q41:	Can string use single quote or double quote?	40
Q42:	Explain type conversions on collection types.	40
Q43:	Explain set theory operations supported by set data type.	40
Q44:	Explain frozenset?	41
Q45:	Explain functions in Python?	41
Q46:	What is a Boolean function?	42
Q47:	Can we specify data type for arguments as well as return types in Python?	42
Q48:	Explain variable arguments?	42
Q49:	Write a program to find occurrences or count of characters in given word.	43
Q50:	What is **kwargs?	43
Q51:	Write a simple Lambda expression?	43
Q52:	Lambda forms in Python contain statements? True or False?	44
Q53:	Explain filter function?	44
Q54:	Explain steps involved in reading and writing a file?	44
Q55:	Explain the term "withstatement"?	45
Q56:	Explain the preferred way of reading a big file?	45
Q57:	Explain modules in Python.	45
Q58:	Explain different ways of importing modules.	45

Q59: Can we create our own module? 46
Q60: Explain in brief about os module and its corresponding functions. 46
Q61: Using os module print the directory structure. 47
Q62: Explain dir function. 47
Q63: Explain exception handling in Python. 48
Q64: How to create user defined exception? 49
Q65: What is the use of raise statement? 49
Q66: How to create own class in Python? Explain constructors. 49
Q67: Is it necessary to have the first argument of class function as self? Can't we rename it to any other variable? 50
Q68: Explain inheritance in Python. 50
Q69: How to determine whether a particular class is sub class? 51
Q70: Does Python support multiple inheritance? 51
Q71: How is diamond problem resolved in case of Python?...51
Q72: Does Python support private method and variables?.....52
Q73: Can __ be used for other purpose than creating private variables or functions? 52
Q74: Does Python support abstract classes? 53
Q75: Differentiate between static methods and class methods in Python. 53
Q76: What are named tuple? 54
Q77: How to sort using lamdas? 54
Q78: Explain Generators? 54
Q79: What is generator expression? 55
Q80: When Python program exits, all the memory is released? Say true or false? 55
Q81: Can a function be passed as parameter to another function? 55
Q82: Can a function be retuned as result from another function? 56
Q83: Explain decorator function. 56

Q84:	How can we represent big text in Python?	58
Q85:	What is PEP 8?	58
Q86:	What is anaconda?	58
Q87:	How to install external modules?	58
Q88:	What is Jupyter notebook?	58
Q89:	What is pickling and unpickling?	59
Q90:	Explain the importance of setup.py?	59
Q91:	Is it possible to make connections to database using Python?	59
Q92:	Explain meta programming?	61
Q93:	Explain Python memory model.	63

3. Numpy Interview Questions 65

Q1:	What is numpy?	65
Q2:	How to install numpy?	65
Q3:	How to create single dimension numpy array?	65
Q4:	Explain different attributes provided by numpy?	66
Q5:	Explain some utility methods provided by numpy for creating different elements?	66
Q6:	How can we change shape of an object?	67
Q7:	Which all data types are supported in Python?	68
Q8:	Explain various simple mathematical operations which can be done on numpy?	68
Q9:	Explain slicing operation in numpy?	69
Q10:	Explain Boolean indexing?	70
Q11:	Perform matrix multiplication using numpy?	71
Q12:	Explain various functions available with numpy?	71
Q13:	What is broadcast?	72
Q14:	Explain rules of broadcasting.	72
Q15:	Explain some statistical measures supported by numpy.	73
Q16:	Explain functions available in numpy.linalg.	75
Q17:	How to save numpy data from memory to flat file?	76
Q18:	What is the use of where and extract?	76

Q19:	What is the use of ndenumerate?	77
Q20:	Explain how can we draw a histogram using numpy?	77

4. Pandas Interview Questions 79

Q1:	What is Pandas?	79
Q2:	How does Pandas represent data?	79
Q3:	How to create Series?	80
Q4:	How to create Data frame?	80
Q5:	How are missing values represented in data frame?	81
Q6:	Explain the process of creating indexes w.r.t. pandas?	81
Q7:	Explain various attributes associated with series.	81
Q8:	Explain various statistical measures supported by pandas.	83
Q9:	Explain reindexing.	86
Q10:	Explain bfill and ffill.	87
Q11:	What all type of iterations are provided in pandas data frame?	87
Q12:	Explain how sorting is supported in pandas?	91
Q13:	How to override default reload option in pandas?	93
Q14:	Explain various slicing options available with pandas?	93
Q15:	Explain advanced statistics with pandas.	95
Q16:	Explain rolling function.	96
Q17:	How can we handle NA in pandas?	97
Q18:	Explain group by function.	98
Q19:	Explain merge functions w.r.t data frame.	100
Q20:	Explain concat method.	101
Q21:	Explain how time related range can be generated in pandas.	102
Q22:	Explain which all data sources can pandas retrieve values.	103
Q23:	Can you compare some of the functions of R and Python?	104

Q24:	How to print a histogram using pandas? 105

5. Scipy and its Applications 107

Q1:	Explain Scipy library. 107
Q2:	Explain how can we perform Normality Tests. 107
Q3:	Explain how can we perform correlation test? 108
Q4:	Explain tests pertaining to Parametric Statistical Hypothesis Tests. 109
Q5:	Explain how to test Nonparametric Statistical Hypothesis Tests. 111
Q6:	Implement logistic regression in Python? 111
Q7:	Explain how to implement decision tree in Python. 111
Q8:	How to implement Random forest in Python? 112
Q9:	How to implement support vector machine in Python? 112
Q10:	Which all kernels are supported by svm in Python? 112
Q11:	Implement KNN algorithm using Python 112
Q12:	How to select k in KNN algorithm? 113
Q13:	How to implement K means in Python? 113
Q14:	How can accuracy of any model be calculated? 113
Q15:	Explain regression metrics. 115
Q16:	Explain how we can print a decision tree or see the rules of the decision tree? 115
Q17:	What is the use of boosting techniques? 116
Q18:	Explain some of the advantages and disadvantages of boosting techniques? 116
Q19:	What is AdaBoost? 117
Q20:	Explain Gradient boosting? 117
Q21:	Explain XGBoost? 118
Q22:	Explain the differences/similarities between bagging and Boosting? 118
Q23:	Write a small snippet to perform operation with neural networks using tensorflow and keras? 119

6. Matplotlib Samples to Remember 121
- Q1: Explain how to draw bar plot. 121
- Q2: How to draw histogram? 122
- Q3: How to draw line chart? 123
- Q4: Draw Pie chart. 123
- Q5: How to get the equation of the line printed line plot? 124
- Q6: Draw scatter plot. 125

7. Statistics with Excel Sheet 127
- Q1: Does Excel has any support for statistics? 127
- Q2: Find correlation using Excel. 128
- Q3: How to get Histogram in excel? 128
- Q4: Explain how to get Descriptive Statistics using Excel. 129
- Q5: Explain how to perform Anova in excel? 130
- Q6: Explain how to perform Rank and Percentile in excel. 131

CHAPTER 1
Data Science Basic Questions and Terms

Note: [Q: Question Number and Ans: Answer]

Q1: Explain the steps involved in data science?

Ans: Following are the steps involved:
  a. Get data from various data sources available.
  b. Generate research question from data.
  c. Identify variables present in data. Also, identify important variables or variables to be analyzed as such.
  d. Generate hypothesis.
  e. Analyze data using graph data like histogram for example.
  f. Fit a model from analyzed data.
  g. Accept or reject the hypothesis.
  h. Research question answer found.

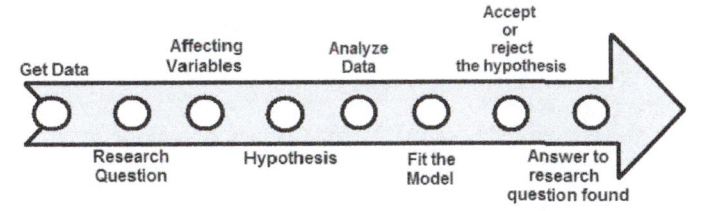

Example of above steps:

a. Get data related to temperature for India reference https://data.gov.in/catalog/annual-and-seasonal-maximum-temperature-india

A template of data set:

"YEAR","ANNUAL","JAN-FEB","MAR-MAY","JUN-SEP","OCT-DEC"
"1901","28.96","23.27","31.46","31.27","27.25"
"1902","29.22","25.75","31.76","31.09","26.49"
"1903","28.47","24.24","30.71","30.92","26.26"
"1904","28.49","23.62","30.95","30.67","26.40"
"1905","28.30","22.25","30.00","31.33","26.57"
"1906","28.73","23.03","31.11","30.86","27.29"
"1907","28.65","24.23","29.92","30.80","27.36"
"1908","28.83","24.42","31.43","30.72","26.64"
"1909","28.39","23.52","31.02","30.33","26.88"
"1910","28.53","24.20","31.14","30.48","26.20"
"1911","28.62","23.90","30.70","31.14","26.31"
"1912","28.95","24.88","31.10","31.15","26.57"
"1913","28.67","24.25","30.89","30.92","26.42"
"1914","28.66","24.59","30.73","30.84","26.40"
"1915","28.94","23.22","31.06","31.51","27.18"
"1916","28.82","24.57","31.88","30.52","26.32"
"1917","28.11","24.52","30.06","30.24","25.74"
"1918","28.66","23.57","30.68","31.11","26.77"

b. Research question, is the annual temperature in India rising?
c. Variable of interest from the above data set ANNUAL.
d. Hypothesis: Temperature is rising.
e. Analyze data from the above data set.

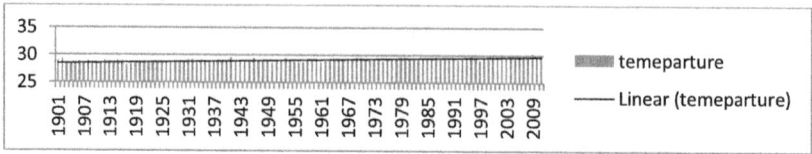

f. Fit the model.
g. Hypothesis accepted or rejected.

Q2: Explain variable and different types of variables?

Ans: Anything which keeps on changing is called variable. Variables are of different type and below are the following:

Dependant/Outcome: A variable being affected, for example annual temperature in above example.

Independent/Predictor: A variable affecting the outcome for e.g. deforestation, pollution, and so on in above example.

Q3: Explain Categorical measurement?

Ans: Categorical measurement contains categories i.e. distinct entities. Example of categories of life on earth is plants, animals, and so on.

Q4: Explain Binary variables?

Ans: Binary variables are those in which only two classes exist, like live or dead, male or female, on or off.

Q5: Explain Nominal measurement?

Ans: Nominal measurements are there more than two classes. Such categories can be numbers too.

Q6: Explain Ordinal variable?

Ans: These are nominal variables which have logical order. Examples include team ranks in cricket or football, merit list of students appearing for grade students.

Q7: Explain Continuous variables?

Ans: These are variables which can take can any value on the measurement scale example includes pitch of voice which can take any possible value within the range.

Q8: Explain Discrete variables?

Ans: These are variables which can take fixed values in range. For example, number of customers in a bank.

Q9: Is it possible to convert continuous values to discrete and vice versa?

Ans: Yes, based upon the motive of study, it is possible to convert discrete values to continuous and vice versa for example, Level of water in tank can take any value in the range and as such a continuous variable.

But we can approximate the same to three different levels like empty, full, or half empty and this now becomes discrete in nature.

Q10: What are interval variables?

Ans: These are variables which are grouped on interval. Example is age can be divided in range like 10-20, 20-30 and so on and, person with particular age would be placed in one of the above groups. When intervals are equal, they represent difference in equal property being measured.

Q11: What are ratio variables?

Ans: This is sub type of interval variables where ratio of scales is used for measurement.

For Example Water representation in chemistry is H_2O which represent two molecules of hydrogen and one molecule of oxygen. Thus, the ratio of elements is 2: 1.

Q12: What are Univariate and Bivariate variables?

Ans: **Univariate variable:** When the variable under consideration is only one then it is called univariate variable study.

Bivariate variable: Involves study of relationship between two variables.

Q13: What is measurement error?

Ans: The discrepancy between the measured value and actual value in terms of number is called measurement error.

For Example While buying fruits from a vendor in kilograms, if we wanted 1 kilogram of fruits and the vendor's weighing machine showed 1 kilogram when we brought the same. After checking the same in another machine, if the measured value shows 0.1 kilogram less than expected then this difference is what we call as measurement error.

Q14: Explain Validity?

Ans: Validity implies whether an instrument measures what it is supposed to measure.

Q15: Explain Reliability?

Ans: Reliability implies whether the instrument gives consistent result across different conditions.

For example, if we test the same value twice on the same entity then the results from the instrument should remain same if it has to be reliable. Such tests are known as test-retest.

Q16: What are the different ways to test hypotheses?

Ans: There are two ways in which hypotheses can be tested:

a. Correlational research
- This is also known as cross-sectional research

- This involves observing the natural pattern or occurrence to test
- Original occurrences are not manipulated

b. Experimental research
- We select the variables of interest
- Then we manipulate some aspect of the environment
- Observe the effect on selected variable

Q17: Explain the different types of variation?

Ans: There are two types in variation explained as follows:

Systematic variation:
- Introduced by experimenter
- The participants are tested under different conditions and the difference in condition is introduced by experimenter

For Example to test use of woolen clothes w.r.t. temperature, we can test a group of 20 people, in both hot and cold climate. Thus, the difference introduced here is in terms of temperature only.

Unsystematic variation:
- Introduced by random factors that exist between the experimental conditions.
- For Example To test use of woolen clothes w.r.t. temperature, we can test a group of 20 people. Of the selected set some might behave differently than expected due to factors like illness and so on.

Q18: Explain repeated-measures design?

Ans: Same measure is measured under different conditions on same set participants.

The difference in two conditions can be caused by the following:
- The manipulation/changes that was carried out on the participants
- Factors that might affect the way in which a participant performs from one time to the next

Q19: What is independent design?

Ans: Same measure is measured under different conditions on different set of participants.

The differences between the two conditions can be caused by the following:

- The manipulation/changes that were carried out on the participants
- Difference in nature or characteristics of participants in each case

Q20: Explain the role of randomization w.r.t variation?

Ans: By using randomization we can ensure that any variation introduced, is due to changes in the conditions/variables introduced rather than any other unexpected changes during the process. Thus, it helps in removing other sources of systematic variation.

Q21: Explain various summary measures.

Ans: **Mode:** Represents the value/score which occurs most frequently in data set.

For example: In the values of occurrences of goal in football by players having T-shirt numbers is as follows:

1, 2, 2, 3, 4, 1, 1, 1, 1, 1, 1

If we arrange it in form of table:

T shirt number	Frequency
1	7
2	2
3	1
4	1

Thus the mode in above example is 1 which happens to have maximum frequency of 7. This can be easily determined from histogram as shown in the following screenshot:

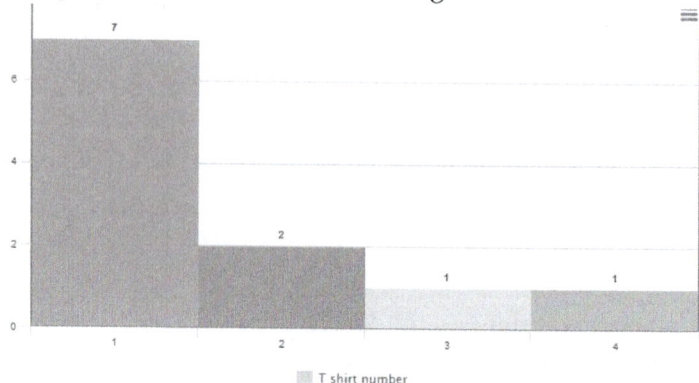

Median: This is the middle value which is obtained by ordering the values/scores in ascending order. If the middle value happens to have two numbers then the average is taken as such:

For example:

Median of 2, 3, 4, 5, 6 happens to be 4.

Median of 2, 3, 4, 5 happens to be average of 3 and 4 which is 3.5.

Median is least affected by outliers.

Mean: Represents mathematical average which is sum of all the elements divided by number of elements.

For example, average strike rate of the batsmen in the game of cricket is the average of strike rates in individual matches.

Range of scores: Subtraction between the maximum value and minimum value in range is called range of scores. This indicates dispersion.

Trimmed mean: Represents the mean after removing extreme cases from both the end i.e. from minimum and maximum end. Both the minimum and maximum values may represent values which are not normal and hence represent outlier. So, while fining trimmed mean, we specify the percentage of values to be ignored from both the ends. Hence, trimmed mean gives better representation of data excluding outlier.

Interquartile range (IQR)

It is a measure of variability, based on dividing a data set into quartiles.

Quartiles are the three values that split the sorted data into four equal parts:

- Q1 is the *middle* value in the first half of the rank-ordered data set
- Q2 is the *median* value in the set
- Q3 is the *middle* value in the second half of the rank-ordered data set

The interquartile range is equal to Q3 minus Q1.

The lower quartile is the median of the lower half of the data.

The upper quartile is the median of the upper half of the data.

Mean absolute deviation: Represents the mean of the absolute value of the deviations from the mean.

Mean absolute deviations from median: Represented by absolute value of the deviations from the median.

Outliers: Represents the value which are not normal or within the range and hence data which is corrupted at the time of capture or due to some other reasons. Since it affects all while finding the mean and other summary values they need to represent this data properly.

Q22: Explain alternate hypotheses and null hypotheses.

Ans: **Alternative hypotheses:** → one you are trying to demonstrate
- Also called experimental hypotheses
- Denoted by H_1
- It assumes that effect as per prediction would exist in the conclusion

Null hypotheses:
- Denoted by H_0
- It assumes that effect as per prediction would not exist in the conclusion
- Thus, this represents opposite of alternative hypotheses

Q23: What is p value?

Ans: It measures the strength of evidence in support of null hypotheses. If this value is less than significance level then null hypotheses is accepted, else rejected.

The range of values that leads the researcher to accept the null hypothesis is called the region of acceptance.

The region other than acceptance is called region of rejection.

Q24: What happens when null hypotheses is rejected?

Ans: When a null hypothesis is rejected, it becomes Type 1 error. The probability of Type 1 error occurring is called significance level.

Q25: Explain directional and non-directional hypotheses.

Ans: **Directional hypotheses:**
- Gives an indication whether the effect which is being studied would grow positively or negatively
- One tailed test is generally used for such cases

Non directional hypotheses:
- Does not give indication of whether the effect which is being studied would grow positively or negatively
- Two tailed test is generally used for such cases

Q26: Explain fit of model?

Ans: It represents the degree till which the determined statistical model represents the data.

Fit of model can represent either under fit, over fit, or perfect fit as such.

A model which is good fit would have low variance between the calculated value and measured value.

Q27: What is relation between sample and population?

Ans: Samples are subset or part of original data or population. If population is very big hence performing analysis on the whole population as such is not easy. Hence, a subset of population data is taken which is known as sample data.

Whether the sample data is true representation of original data set considered is determined with the help of estimation, confidence interval, and so on.

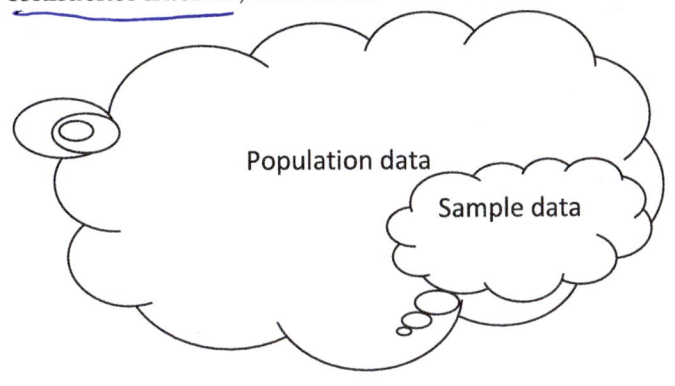

Population data

Sample data

Q28: What is estimation?

Ans: By using information available from sample, we can make inferences w.r.t. population, which is what is known as estimation. Parameters used are mean, standard deviation, and so on.

Q29: Explain deviation score?

Ans: This is defined as the difference between actual score/value and mean.

Q30: Explain variance?

Ans: Variance is the average error between the mean and the measured values.

It indicates the difference between the average value calculated and the observed value as such.

It is an indication of how different individuals in group differ or vary from each other.

The population variance is given:
$$PV = \Sigma (X_i - X)^2 / N$$

- PV is the population variance
- X is the population mean
- X_i is the ith element from the population
- N is the number of elements in the population

The sample variance is given by:
$$SV = \Sigma (x_i - x)^2 / (n - 1)$$

- SV is the sample variance
- x is the sample mean
- x_i is the ith element from the sample
- n is the number of elements in the sample

Q31: Explain Standard deviation.

Ans: Square root of the variance is also called standard deviation. This is done to keep the measurement same as original one. They indicate the nearness of the points measured w.r.t. mean. Smaller the standard deviation will be more nearer to mean and vice versa.

Q32: Explain standard error.

Ans: Standard error indicates how well a sample represents the original population. When we break the original population into various small samples, we would like to know the difference between the sample considered and original population. This is represented by standard error.

The smaller the standard error, the closer or true representation of original population.

$$SE = \Sigma \text{ (sample mean - overall population mean)}^2 / \text{ (number of samples)}$$

Q33: What is precision?

Ans: It refers to the closeness between estimates from different samples. Thus indicating the opposite of standard error and are inversely related to Standard error.

Q34: Explain confidence intervals.

Ans: This indicates the boundaries in which the mean value will fall.

It is a range of scores constructed, such that the population mean will fall within.

They are limits constructed such that for a certain percentage of the time the true value of the population mean will fall within these range.

Q35: Explain confidence level. → eg 95% confidence level.

Ans: Refers to the percentage of all possible samples that can be expected to include the true population parameter.

Q36: Explain alpha.

Ans: Alpha is defined as 1-confidence interval. This implies probability that the true value remains outside the confidence interval. If confidence interval is 99% then alpha is 1-99% which is 0.01.

Q37: Explain Beta.

Ans: The probability of committing Type 2 error is called beta. Type 2 error is one in which a rejected null hypotheses is accepted. The probability of avoiding Type 2 error is called power of test.

Q38: Explain Accuracy.

Ans: It indicates how much does sample value or parameters matches with the population statistic. If the value of mean of both sample and population are exactly equal then we can say that the sample is fully accurate. If not fully equal then we say that sample is accurate by n limit where n is the difference between sample and population.

Q39: Explain Bias.

Ans: Bias indicates whether the estimation of sample is over fit or under fit w.r.t. population data. For e.g. if the population mean is 4 and sample mean calculated is 3 then this is under estimate bias. Such estimate in which both sample and population parameter is not equal are called bias estimate.

Q40: What is central limit theorem?

Ans: It states that the distribution of the mean of any independent, random variable can be approximated to normal if the sample size is large enough.

Generally, the sample size of above 30 or sometimes 40 is taken as reference.

This all ows us to approximate bigger samples to normal distribution without having to take hundreds or thousands of distribution.

Standard Normal distribution is preferred as such because mean is equal to zero and variance is one.

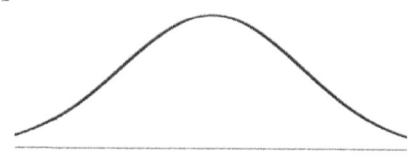

Q41: Explain Absolute value?

Ans: Absolute value is positive value or magnitude irrespective of its initial sign.

Q42: What is degree of freedom?

Ans: It is equal to the number of independent observations in a sample minus number of population parameters to be estimated.

Q43: Explain cluster sampling.

Ans: In this method the number of clusters or groups to be formed as pre decided (generally denoted by N) from population data.

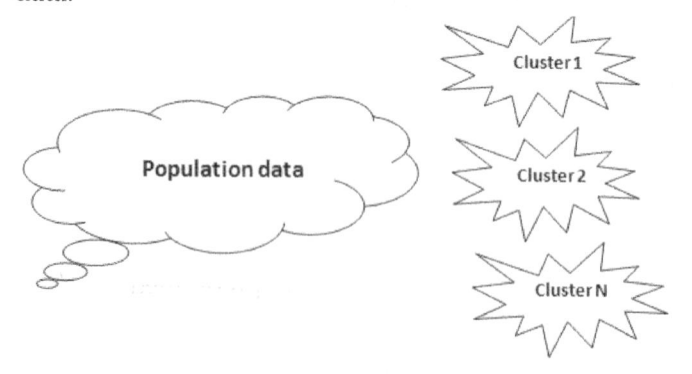

The number of elements in each cluster is known and each element from population data is assigned to one cluster. For e.g. clustering can be done on attributes like customer state.

Sampling can be further classified as:

- **One-stage sampling:** All of the elements within selected clusters are included in the sample.

- **Two-stage sampling:** A subset of elements within selected clusters is randomly selected.

Q44: Explain Correlation coefficients?

Ans: Correlation indicates the relationship between two variables.
- As such variables can be positively correlated in which positive change in one variable effect the other variable positively.
- If variables are negatively correlated the positive change in one variable affects the other variable negatively.
- The formula for above is given by:
  Correlation co-efficient = $\Sigma(xy) / sqrt[(\Sigma x^2) * (\Sigma y^2)]$, where x and y are variables under consideration.
- The value of correlation co-efficient ranges from -1 to +1.

Q45: Explain sample space.

Ans: The outcomes of any statistical experiment are denoted by sample space. Any outcome from such space is called sample point. One or more sample point is called event. When events do not have any sample point in common they are known as mutually exclusive event.

Q46: What is non parametric algorithm?

Ans: Non parametric algorithm does not make any assumptions on data distribution.

Q47: How can learning be classified?

Ans: Following are the classifications:
- **Supervised:**
  o Data is clearly labeled and the algorithms learn to predict the output from the input data
  o Offline analysis of data possible
  o The number of classes are predefined
  o Accuracy is high
  o Examples include classification and regression
- **Unsupervised:**
  o Much amount of data is unlabeled and the algorithms learn to inherent structure from the input data
  o Analysis is on real time data
  o Number of classes may be unknown

- o   Accuracy ranges from moderate to high
- o   Examples include Clustering and Association
- **Semi-supervised:**
  - o   A mixture of data having label and no labels forms this one
  - o   Can be considered as intermediate to above two

Q48: What is classification?

Ans: Classification predictive modeling is the task of approximating a mapping function (f) from input variables (X) to discrete output variables (y).

The output variables are often called labels or categories.

The mapping function predicts the class or category for a given observation.

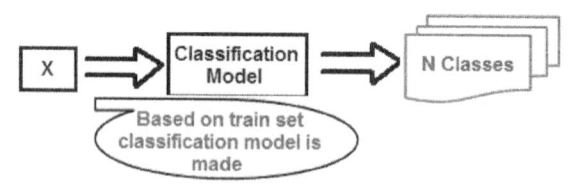

```
X → Classification Model → N Classes
      Based on train set classification model is made
```

Q49: Explain the steps involved in classification.

Ans:

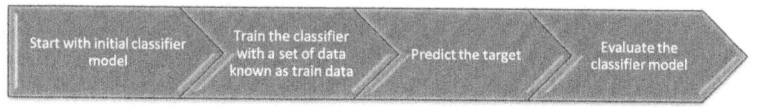

Start with initial classifier model → Train the classifier with a set of data known as train data → Predict the target → Evaluate the classifier model

Q50: What is regression?

Ans: Regression predictive modeling is the task of approximating a mapping function (f) from input variables (X) to a continuous output variable (y).

A continuous output variable can be a real-value, such as an integer or floating point value and be any measures such as size amount, and so on.

Error indicates the difference between actual value and predicted value in case of regression mostly root mean square error is used w.r.t. regression.

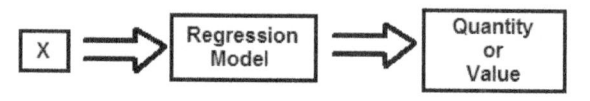

```
X → Regression Model → Quantity or Value
```

Q51: Explain the similarities and differences between Classification and Regression.

Ans: Differences between classification and regression:

Classification	Regression
Predicts classes	Predicts quantity
Can be evaluated using accuracy	Can be evaluated using RMSE (root mean square error)
Discrete class label is the output	Continuous quantity is the output

The similarities are that both try to make prediction based on input values.

Q52: Explain various terms encountered during classification algorithm.

Ans: Classifier is an algorithm that maps the input data to a specific category.

Classification model: After analyzing input data, a classification model is made. The model can take new data as input and predict the class labels/categories.

Feature: A feature is an individual measurable property of a phenomenon being observed.

Binary Classification: Classification task with two possible outcomes.

Multi class classification: Classification with more than two classes is involved. In multi class classification each sample is assigned to one and only one target label.

E.g. an item can be classified as fruit or vegetable not both.

Multi label classification: Classification task where each sample is mapped to a set of target labels having more than one class.

Example: A fruit can be classified as sweet and sour both.

Q53: Explain multi class classification?

Ans: Whenever we have more than two, that is, three or more classes to classify it is called multi class classification. This is also known as a multi nominal classification.

By default, all the algorithms of scipy are multi class.

Some of the strategies involved are:

One vs. rest (One vs. all) trains a single classifier per class. The samples that match with the class are positive, and that which does not match is negative.

One vs. One:
- We pick a pair of classes from a set of n classes
- Develop a binary classifier for each selected pair
- For n classes, all possible combinations of pairs of classes from n are selected
- Then, for each pair, we develop a binary support vector machine (SVM)

Q54: Explain multi label classification?

Ans: Whenever we have more than one target variables associated with a problem, we call that as multi label classification.

For example: While classifying fruit, we can classify it as fruit, sweet, red-colored, and so on. As we can clearly see, we have assigned multi labels to the same object.

Q55: Explain how multi label problem can be solved?

Ans: Following are different ways in which it can be achieved:

Binary relevance: In this technique, we treat each label as a separate single class classification problem.

Achieved with the help of skmultilearn.problem_transform. BinaryRelevance sample:

```
fromskmultilearn.problem_transform import BinaryRelevance
classifier = BinaryRelevance(any model)
```

Classifier Chains: A chain of a classifier is formed in which input passed to the first classifier is trained and passed on to the next classifier and so on.

skmultilearn.problem_transform.ClassifierChain is used for this purpose:

```
fromskmultilearn.problem_transform import ClassifierChain
classifier = ClassifierChain(model)
```

Label power set: In this we try to form a single model which would try to solve the multi class model problem.

skmultilearn.problem_transform.LabelPowerset is used:

```
fromskmultilearn.problem_transform import LabelPowerset
classifier = LabelPowerset(model)
```

Q56: Explain some important metrics with respect to testing a model?

Ans: True positive indicates that the model was able to predict the positive outcome correctly. It indicates that the model is able to identify the condition when the condition is present.

True negative indicates the model is able to properly predict the negative class. It indicates that the model does not find the condition when the condition is not present.

False positive indicates the model wrongly predicts the positive class. It indicates that the model finds or reports a condition when the condition is not present.

False negative indicates the model wrongly predicts the negative class. It indicates that the model does not report a condition when it is actually present.

All the four conditions are easily indicated by confusion metrics:

	condition present	condition absent
positive	true positive	false positive
negative	false negative	true negative

Figure 1

Recall /Sensitivity / True Positive Rate (also known as TPR) ability to determine the condition when the condition is present. It can be found by:

True Positive/ (True Positive + False Negative)

Specificity/ True Negative Rate (also known as TNR): It indicates the ability to not detect the condition when the condition is not actually present. It can be found by

True Negative/ (True Negative + False Positive)

Precision/ Predictive value positive: This indicates the number of items correctly identified as positive from total items True Positive/ (True Positive + False Positive)

False Positive Rate or Type I Error: Number of items which are wrongly identified as positive from total true negatives

False Positive/ (False Positive + True Negative)

False Negative Rate or Type II Error: This indicates the number of items wrongly identified as negative out of total true positives

False Negative/ (False Negative + True Positive)

Q57: What is logistic regression?

Ans: Logistic regression also known as logit model is most useful for understanding the influence of several independent variables on a single outcome variable.

Function representation:

$$p = 1/1 + e^{-(\beta 0 + \beta 1 X1 + \beta 2 X2 ... \beta n Xn)}$$

It is a kind of predictive analysis.

In this algorithm, the probabilities describing the possible outcomes of a single trial are modeled using a logistic function.

Disadvantages:

Assumes all predictors are independent of each other which may not always be true.

Works only when the predicted or output variable is binary.

Q58: Explain Naïve Bayes.

Ans: Naive Bayes algorithm based on Bayes' theorem with the assumption of independence between every pair of features. This implies the predictors are independent of each other.

Let **P(c|x)** is the posterior probability of class (c, target) given predictor (x, attributes).

P(c) is the prior probability of class.

P(x|c) is the likelihood which is the probability of predictor given class.

P(x) is the prior probability of predictor.

$$P(c|x) = \frac{P(x|c)P(c)}{P(x)}$$

- Likelihood: $P(x|c)$
- Class Prior Probability: $P(c)$
- Posterior Probability: $P(c|x)$
- Predictor Prior Probability: $P(x)$

$$P(c|X) = P(x_1|c) \times P(x_2|c) \times \cdots \times P(x_n|c) \times P(c)$$

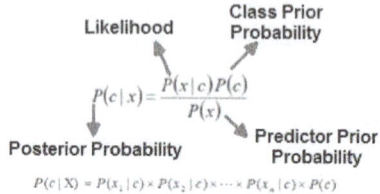

Advantages:

- Are extremely fast
- Training set required is less

- Performs well for categorical values

Disadvantages:
- Zero frequency problems will occur if some of the categories is missed and as a result the effect of same would be neglected
- Assumes independence of predictors which is not always true in real world

Q59: What is Stochastic Gradient Descent?

Ans: Gradient is an effective method to calculate parameters or co-efficient which would cause the cost to minimum. The process involves assuming some value as co-efficient and keeping on calculating the slope and adjusting the co-efficient till a minimum cost is found.

But when the logic is applied on very large data set, it becomes slow. Stochastic Gradient Descent is used for this purpose. In this, calculation is done based on batch instances rather than at the end.

Advantages:
- The algorithm is extremely effective
- Easy to use

Disadvantages:
- Requires large number of parameters

Q60: Explain decision tree algorithm.

Ans: Decision tree

Generates the set of rules which depends on attributes or features and based upon classes.

A decision tree is an inverse tree.

The node at the top is called root node and the one without any child is called leaves.

Each part of decision tree represents something which is indicated:
- Each attribute/feature is represented by node
- Rule or decision is represented by link
- Leaf node or node without children represents an the output class

It uses a recursive approach.

The aim is to divide the given data to various groups or classes based upon cost function.

Classification and Regression trees are also known as **CART**.

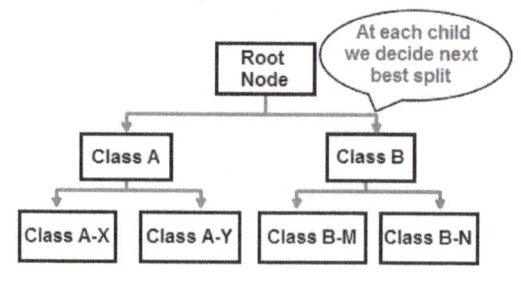

```
                    ┌─────────────┐
                    │    Root     │  At each child
                    │    Node     │  we decide next
                    └─────────────┘  best split
                      ↙         ↘
              ┌─────────┐   ┌─────────┐
              │ Class A │   │ Class B │
              └─────────┘   └─────────┘
               ↙     ↘       ↙     ↘
         ┌───────┐ ┌───────┐ ┌───────┐ ┌───────┐
         │Class  │ │Class  │ │Class  │ │Class  │
         │ A-X   │ │ A-Y   │ │ B-M   │ │ B-N   │
         └───────┘ └───────┘ └───────┘ └───────┘
```

Advantages:
- Requires small data preparation
- Simple to understand and visualize
- Can handle dataset which can contain numbers
- Can handle dataset which can contain data in the form of categories

Disadvantages:

Outliers can have severe effect on output. Changes in input data does have an important effect on output.

Q61: What is Gini index?

Ans: The Gini index is the cost function used to evaluate splits in the dataset.

It gives the measure of impurity.

How effective is the split of data based upon features can be easily determined by Gini index.

A Gini score of 0 is ideal expected result while one having half-half probability is not preferred.

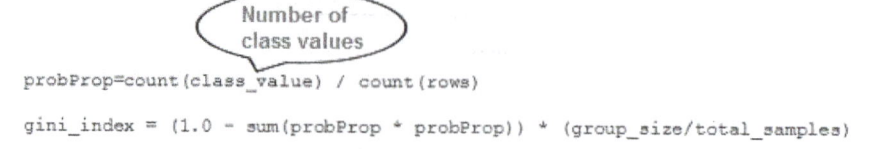

```
probProp=count(class_value) / count(rows)        [Number of class values]

gini_index = (1.0 - sum(probProp * probProp)) * (group_size/total_samples)
```

Q62: Is Gini index the only means which can be used in decision tree?

Ans: Entrophy is another measure which can be used with decision tree.

Q63: What is Pruning w.r.t. decision tree?

Ans: Pruning refers to the removal of branches having low importance in terms of classification or regression. The advantages are reduced complexity and reducing over fitting.

The algorithm basically calculates whether removing a particular node causes an impact on prediction precision of the tree.

Q64: What is random forest?

Ans: Random forest is a meta-estimator that fits a number of decision trees.

It makes use of average to improve the ability to predict the model.

The output from each decision tree is used to finally predict the final model and for doing this, it makes use of majority voting. The data is classified on the class which has majority voting.

To generate this forest, sub samples are used and using sub samples from original data set sub trees are created.

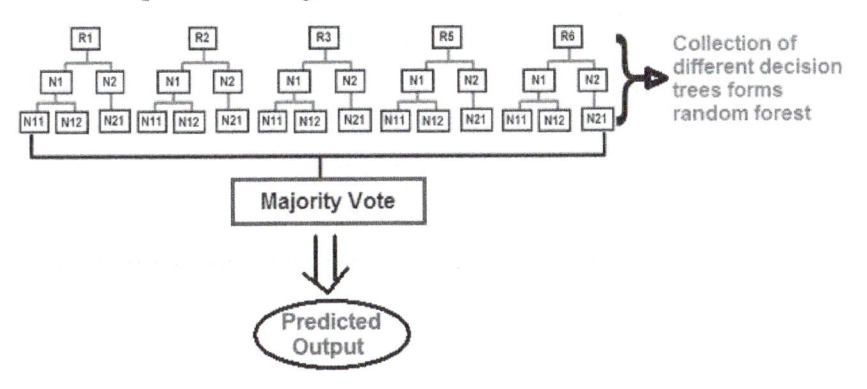

Advantages: Over fitting is reduced.

Disadvantages: It's slow as real time updates take time.

Q65: Explain the difference between Random forest and decision tree.

Ans:

Decision tree	Random Forest
Is a subpart of Random forest	Consists of lot of decision tree
Over fitting can occur	Over fitting is avoided
Faster	Slower
Easy to interpret	Difficult to interpret

Q66: What is overfitting and underfitting?

Ans: Following is the explanation for overfitting and underfitting:

Overfitting:
- Refers to a model which performs very well w.r.t. training set. Such model is able to predict the noise and randomness w.r.t. training set very well but would not perform well when it comes to newly arrived data.
- Occurs with nonparametric and nonlinear models.

Underfitting:
- Refers to a model that does not perform well both with training set and newly arrived data.
- An underfitted model would be directly rejected due to its performance via benchmark and accuracy.

Q67: What are the reasons for under fitting occurrences?

Ans: Under fitting is said to happen when a model is unable to capture or understand the nature of data. This has a direct impact on the accuracy of the model.

The reason for this could be:
- Less data available to analyze
- Wrong data
- Wrong features considered
- It could be also be due to wrong formed model

The solution to under fitting is to make use of more data and possibly even clean data by removing unwanted features or columns.

Shown below is how under fitting looks when plotted

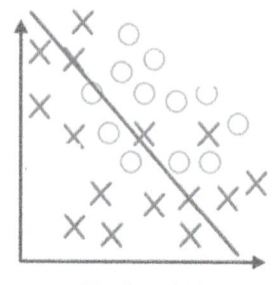

Under-fitting

Figure 2

Q68: Does over fitting get affected by noise?

Ans: Over fitting is said to happen when a model gets easily affected by noise or outliers.

The details available in such a case are more, and as a result of this, model gets affected.

Following is the over fitting diagram when plotted:

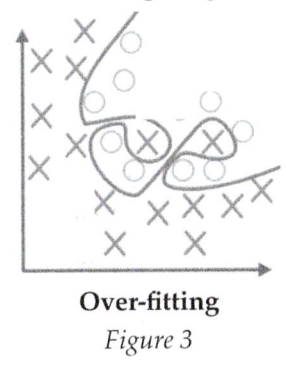

Over-fitting
Figure 3

Over fitting can be overcome by:

- **Pruning:** Pruning as the name suggests, is cutting. We prune wanted data in addition to nodes that gets easily affected by wrong data.
- **Cross-Validation:** Sample prediction error is one way that helps on the problem of over fitting. This is generally accomplished with the help of k fold validation. In k fold validation, the original sample data is categorized into k subsets. One of the samples is used for testing, and remaining subsets are used to form the model. The output results which would be collected and then averaged out get the final estimation.
- **Regularization:** The aim of this is to find out features that align with the objective of the problem and thus removing features that do not contribute to the final output.

Q69: Explain KNN (K Nearest Neighbour) steps involved, advantage and disadvantage.

Ans: KNN abbreviation is K Nearest Neighbor and is explained down below:
- Not an eager learner i.e. learns lazily
- It stores instances of training set.
- The output is determined by majority vote which is given

by k nearest neighbors of each point.

Steps involved are as follows:

a. Calculate the distance.

b. Find the closest neighbors.

c. Vote for labels.

Advantages:

- Much faster.
- No need to train a model for generalization.
- Can be used for nonlinear data and regression problems.

Disadvantages:

- Large memory foot print.
- Performance decreases with increase in number of dimensions.

Q70: **Explain selection bias.**

Ans: Selection bias is the bias introduced by the selection of individuals, groups or data for analysis in such a way that proper randomization is not achieved, thereby ensuring that the sample obtained is not representative of the population intended to be analyzed.

They are systematic in nature and produced by the measurement or sampling process.

Q71: **What does selection bias indicate w.r.t. algorithm?**

Ans: It indicates that some important variable has been left off or not considered during the algorithm.

Q72: **What is Bootstrap sample?**

Ans: Bootstrap sample is used to estimate the distribution. A sample taken with replacement from an observed data set is called bootstrap sample.

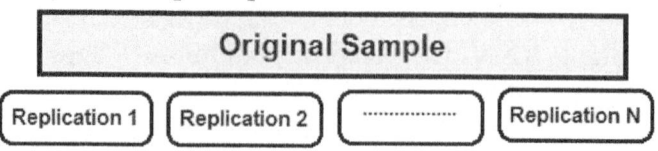

```
        ┌─────────────────────────────────┐
        │         Original Sample         │
        └─────────────────────────────────┘
   ┌─────────────┐ ┌─────────────┐ ┌ ─ ─ ─ ─ ┐ ┌─────────────┐
   │Replication 1│ │Replication 2│  ........   │Replication N│
   └─────────────┘ └─────────────┘ └ ─ ─ ─ ─ ┘ └─────────────┘
```

Q73: **What is Resampling?**

Ans: Resampling combines shuffling and bootstrapping.

Q74: **Explain tail.**

Ans: Tail is the portion of frequency distribution where extreme values are observed at a very low frequency.

Q75: **Explain the difference between one way test and two way test.**

Ans: **One-way test**

It is the hypothesis test where results occur only in one direction.

Two-way test

It is the hypothesis test where results occur in two directions.

Q76: **Explain degree of freedom.**

Ans: It indicates how much value from given samples are supposed to vary to give the required result.

In a sample of 5 we can say 4 values can vary if the mean is known and 4 values are known.

Q77: **What is predictive modeling?**

Ans: Prediction modeling involves building a model which will allow predicting a result/events/behavior whether value of input variables are given. To find out the relationship of input variables and how they affect the output forms the part of regression study.

Q78: **What is time series analysis?**

Ans: Analysis which makes use of data in a particular time interval or periods is called time series analysis. Temporal aspects continue in this type of analysis. It may involve observation of a variable at different time instances (time series data) or collecting different data at same point of time (cross sectional data) or a combination of both (pooled data).

Q79: **What is deep learning?**

Ans: Deep learning makes it possible to learn by existing examples. The models are generated by computer by using existing examples.

The underlying relationship of data can be determined with the help of neural network

Neural network consists of various nodes or computers interconnected to perform complex/vast computation.

To achieve deep learning we require large amount of labeled

data set as well as large computing capability.

Again, deep learning is a part of machine learning where the scale of operation is much higher.

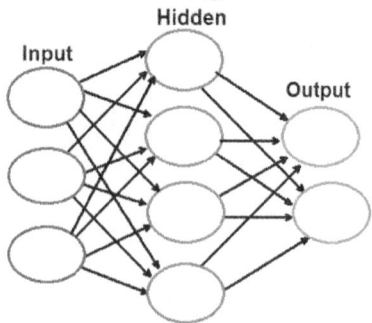

Q80: **What is Convolutional Neural Network?**

Ans: CNN or ConvNet stands for Convolutional neural network, is a type of learning in which model learns to perform classification of models. It eliminates the need to perform manual feature extraction. It allows this with the help of many layers many of which can be hidden.

Q81. **What are different ways to determine optimal value of clusters?**

Ans: **Elbow method:** makes use of sum of squares of each cluster is calculated. The calculated values is then plotted in the form of graph. The best solution is selected based on graph by looking at the slope

Gap method: This makes use of gap value which is determined by looking at the variation between clusters for various values of k under null reference

Silhouette method: makes use of silhouette average to compute the best performing cluster. The above average is determined by looking at consistency within cluster

Q82. **What are various distance related functions for similarity measures?**

Ans: Some of the common ones are Euclidean Distance, Cosine Similarity, Pearson's Coefficient and Jaccard Similarity.

CHAPTER 2
Python Programming Questions

Note: [Q: Question Number and Ans: Answer]

Q1: **Is Python Object oriented?**
Ans: Yes, Python is an object oriented programming language since we can deal with classes and objects.

Q2: **Is Python case sensitive?**
Ans: Yes

Q3: **What kind of language is Python?**
Ans: Python is interpreted programming language.

Q4: **What are different versions of Python?**
Ans: Python comes with two major versions 2.x and 3.x.
There are lots of differences between both of them. Following are some of them:

Command/Syntax	Python 3	Python 2
Division 1/3	1/3	0
Print syntax	print("hello")	print "hello"
Type representation type(int)	<class 'type'>	<type 'type'>
Range generation function	Xrange	range
Unicode difference	Supports utf-8 string, bytearray and byte	Supports ASCII str() and uniciode function
Preferred input function	Input	raw_input
Raising Exceptions (syntax difference)	raise MyError("some error")	raise MyError, " some error "
Handling Exceptions (syntax difference)	except MyError as err:	except MyError, err:
Return type as iterable objects instead of list	Supported in 3 For example: • filter() • zip() • map() • dictionary's .keys(), .values() and .items() method	Returns list instead of iterators

Q5: Explain different implementations of Python?

Ans: Following are different implementations:

- **CPython:** Reference implementation written in C and native Python.
- **Stackless Python:** is an addition or improvement over CPython to support micro threads.
- **PyPy:** is just in time compiler where program is executed on fly rather than compile time.
- MicroPython and CircuitPython supports Microcontrollers.
- Jython compiles into Java byte code, which can then be executed by every Java virtual machine implementation.
- IronPython allows running Python programs on the .NET Common Language Runtime.
- The RPython language can be compiled to C, Java bytecode, or Common Intermediate Language, and is used to build the PyPy interpreter of Python.
- Pyjs compiles Python to JavaScript.

- Cython compiles Python to C and C++.
- Pythran compiles Python to C++.

Q6: Is Python loosely typed?

Ans: Python is loosely typed programming language since the same variable can hold different data at different points of time.

For example:
```
a = 20 (holds int)
a = "rahul" (holds string now)
```

Same variable can be used to store different value or data belonging to different data types.

Q7: How to start a new block in Python?

Ans: A new block begins when the line is intended by 4 spaces.

Q8: How to get data type of a particular variable?

Ans: Type function is used in the data type of enclosed variable.

For example:
```
>>> a = 10
>>> type(a)
<class 'int'>
```

Q9: How many ways can Python program be run?

Ans: Python programs can be run using IDLE which is the integrated IDE or it can also be run from outside using **python.exe** in windows or **python.sh** in UNIX/LINUX based environment.

Q10: Explain the importance of Pylint and Pychecker.

Ans: Pylint is used to check coding standards w.r.t. modules.

Pychecker is a static analysis tool that helps find out bugs in the source code.

Q11: Explain Zen of Python.

Ans: Long time Pythoneer Tim Peters succinctly channels the BDFL's guiding principles for Python's design into 20 aphorisms, only 19 of which have been written down.

The Zen of Python

Beautiful is better than ugly.

Explicit is better than implicit.

Simple is better than complex.

Complex is better than complicated.
Flat is better than nested.
Sparse is better than dense.
Readability counts.
Special cases aren't special enough to break the rules.
Although practicality beats purity.
Errors should never pass silently.
Unless explicitly silenced.
In the face of ambiguity, refuse the temptation to guess.
There should be one-- and preferably only one --obvious way to do it.
Although that way may not be obvious at first unless you're Dutch.
Now is better than never.
Although never is often better than *right* now.
If the implementation is hard to explain, it's a bad idea.
If the implementation is easy to explain, it may be a good idea.
Namespaces are one honking great idea – let's do more of those!

Q12: How to print Zen in Python?

Ans: We can print Zen of Python by using:
```
import this
print(this)
```

Q13: Explain Python data types.

Ans:
- **Integers:** Represent numbers without decimals
- **Floating point:** Represent number with decimals
- Complex numbers represents numbers having real and imaginary part
- String collection of characters
- Boolean represents the value as True or False

For example:
```
a = 5
print(a, "belongs to this type", type(a))
a = 2.0
print(a, "belongs to this type", type(a))
```

```
a = 1+2j
print(a , " has type",type(a))
a = 'Hello world`
print(a," has type",type(a))
a = True
print(a , " has type",type(a))
a = 1+2j
print("Is complex number?",
isinstance(a,complex))
```

Output:

5 belongs to this type <class 'int'>
2.0 belongs to this type <class 'float'>
(1+2j) has type <class 'complex'>
Hello world has type <class 'str'>
True has type <class 'bool'>
Is complex number? True

Q14: How can we switch variables in Python?

Ans:
```
a = 'Hello'
b = 'World'
print(a, b)
a, b = b, a
print(a, b)
```
Value of a and b are interchanged here

Q15: What is the use of pass statement in Python?

Ans: Pass statement indicates no operation statement. It is generally used to complete the body of classes or functions for alter use.

Q16: Is Python pass by value or pass by reference?

Ans: Neither of them is used.

Python passes arguments by value where all values are references to actual objects.

Q17: Does Python supports chained operations?

Ans: Yes, chained operations are supported by Python.
```
no = 8
if 16 > no > 2:
    print("Chained comparison ")
```

In the above example, 16 is compared with 8 which is further compared with 2.

Q18: **Explain ALL and ANY.**

Ans: ALL returns TRUE, only when all the conditions are TRUE. Any return TRUE even when one condition is TRUE.

```
lst= range(20)
print(all(value > 18 for value in lst)) # returns false since range starts with 0
lst = range(21,100)
print(all(value > 18 for value in lst)) # returns true because range starts with 21
print(any(value > 18 for value in lst)) # returns true since 22 is greater than 18 and is true
print(any(value < 18 for value in lst)) # return false since not a single value exists which satisfies given
    #condition
```

Q19: **Explain the difference between IS and ==.**

Ans: **IS:** True only if 2 variables point to same object.

==: True if objects which are referred by objects are equal.

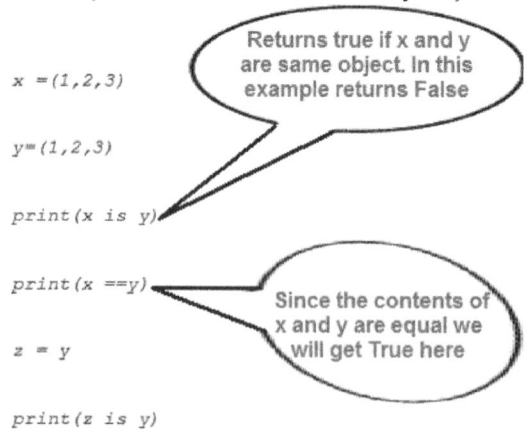

```
x =(1,2,3)

y=(1,2,3)

print(x is y)
```
Returns true if x and y are same object. In this example returns False

```
print(x ==y)

z = y
```
Since the contents of x and y are equal we will get True here

```
print(z is y)
```

Q20: **Explain supported collection of data type w.r.t. Python?**

Ans: Python supports four collections of data types:

List:
- Stores data in a fashion similar to array in other programming language.

- It is mutable and item can be added subtracted or deleted.
- Index starts with zero.
- [] is used to indicate that collection is list.
- It can be homogenous and heterogeneous i.e. store data of same or different data type.
- It can contain duplicates.

Tuples:
- Immutable collection i.e. changes to elements are not possible.
- Indicated by ().
- Again can be homogenous and heterogeneous i.e. store data of same or different data type.
- Duplicates can be present.

Set:
- Duplicates are absent in set.
- It makes use of {} symbol.

Dictionary:
- Stores data in form of key value pair.
- Indicated by {} with each item having : between
- Key has to be immutable object.

Q21: Create a simple number list?

Ans: a = [1,22,33]

Above creates a simple list having three values.

Index	Value
0	1
1	22
2	33

Q22: Can you create nested list?

Ans: Following is a nested list of three elements having list again at index 1 and nested list at location 2:
- nestedLst = ["hello", [100,101], ['aAA',['pAA','rAA']]]
- print(' Nested list',nestedLst)
- print(nestedLst[0])# prints hello
- print(nestedLst[2][1][1])) # prints rAA

Q23: Explain CRUD (Create, Update, and Delete) operations from list.

Ans: **Creation:**
```
lst = [11,22,33, 44]
```
Above statement creates a list with the name lst.

Empty list creation:
```
lst =[]
```
The above statement creates an empty list.

Adding single element in list:
```
lst.append(55)
```

Adding elements of another list:
```
lst.extend([44,44,33])
```

Concatenate list:

Concatenate is to join two list.

Following code adds two list and creates a new list c containing elements from both list.
```
a =[1,2,3,4]
b=[5,65]
c = a + b
print(c) #Outputs 1,2,3,4,5,65
```

Remove element using value:
```
a =[1,2,3,4]
a.remove(3)
print(a) #[1,2,4]
```
In above code, element with value 3 is removed.

Delete elements by using index:
```
a =[1,2,3,4]
del a[2] #removes element at index 2
print(a) #[1,2,4]
```

Clear or Empty a list:
```
a=[1,2,3,4]
a.clear()
print(a) # prints []
```

Length of list:
```
To print size of list len, function is used.
a=[1,2,3,4]
print( len(a)) #prints 4
```

Q24: Explain operations in dictionary.

Ans: **Creation:**
```
sdict ={1:`one`,2:`two`}
```
The above statement creates a dictionary of two items having keys 1 and 2 and corresponding values as one and two respectively.

Creation of empty
```
sdict={}
Add key value pair
sdict={}
sdict[3] =`three`
```
The above statement adds an item in the dictionary with the key as 3 and value as three.

Add or Update elements from another dictionary

Addition of new elements from another dictionary.
```
dict1 ={1:`one`,2:`two`}
dict2 ={5:`five`}
dict1.update(dict2)
print(dict1)  //prints 1:one,2:two,5:five
```
Updating of existing element from another dictionary.
```
dict1 ={1:`one`,2:`two`,5:`FIVE`}
dict2 ={5:`five`}
dict1.update(dict2)
print(dict1) # 1:one 2: two 5: five
```
In the above example the value of key 5 is replaced from FIVE to five.

Thus, update is taken from dict2.

Clear or Empty dictionary
```
dict1 ={1:`one`,2:`two`,5:`FIVE`}
dict1.clear()
print(dict1) #prints {}
Length of dictionary
len(dict) get length of dictionary
```

Q25: Explain operation with tuples.

Ans: **Creation**
```
tup = (3, 4)
```
Creation of empty tuple:
```
tup = ()
```

Creation of tuple with single element

This is a bit of challenge because since (1) is taken as number as compared to tuple.

So, to create tuple with one element we make use of the following:

```
tup = (1,)
```

Adding new elements or removing elements from tuples are not possible since tuples are immutable.

Length of tuples:

```
len(a)
```

Q26: Explain del?

Ans: The del is used to remove variables from memory.

```
a= (1,2,3)
print(a) #prints 1 2 3
del a
print(a) # gives a not defined error
```

Q27: If del can remove variable can it remove tuple variable?

Ans: Yes, **del** can remove tuple variable. A tuple has to be immutable till it lives in memory. While **del** removes the object or variable from memory itself hence **del** can remove tuple.

```
a = (1,2)
del a
```

But if we try to remove an element from tuple using del, it won't work.

```
a = (1,2)
del a[2]  #TypeError: 'tuple' object doesn't
support item deletion
```

Q28: Delete last element in a list.

Ans:

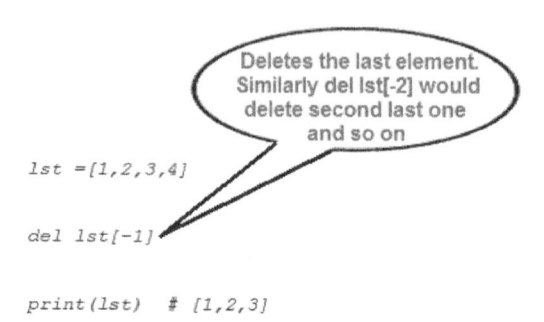

```
lst =[1,2,3,4]

del lst[-1]
```

Deletes the last element. Similarly del lst[-2] would delete second last one and so on

```
print(lst)  # [1,2,3]
```

Q29: Predict the output of following code.
```
a = (1,2,3,4)
b= (5,65)
c = a + b
print(c)
```
Ans: This question is tricky, mainly because it involves tuples which are immutable. So, the general answer given by many is, it would raise an error which is incorrect. The above code adds two tuples to generate new tuple. Existing tuples are untouched which satisfies immutability property. Hence, output is

(1, 2, 3, 4, 5, 65). So, while reading such questions see if the immutability is affected or not. If not then operation would be successful.

Q30: What do you mean by list comprehension?
Ans: The process of creating a list while performing some operation on the data so that it can be accessed using an iterator is referred to as list comprehension.

Q31: Explain the preferred way for looping through list?
Ans: The preferred way of looping through list is with the help of enumerate function.

Enumerate function returns index and corresponding value:

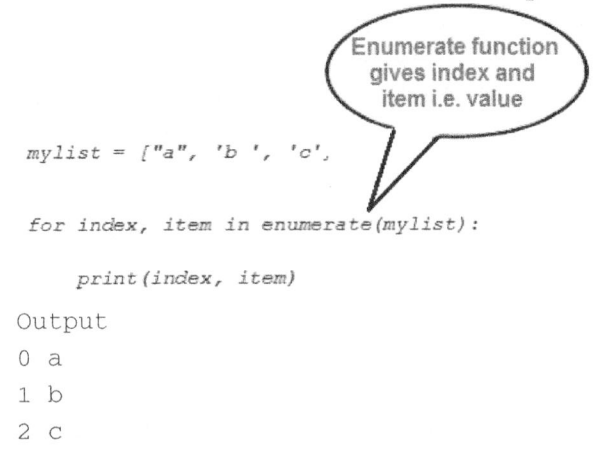

```
mylist = ["a", 'b ', 'c',

for index, item in enumerate(mylist):
     print(index, item)
```

(Enumerate function gives index and item i.e. value)

Output
0 a
1 b
2 c

Q32: Find the reverse of the dictionary?
Ans: Reverse of dictionary means key becomes value and value becomes the key.

It is easily achievable in Python.

```
countryDict={1:'UK',2:'USA'}
```
Key and value are interchanged here. For each key value pair we interchange to form value key pair

```
reversed_dict = {value: key for key, value in countryDict.items()}

print(reversed_dict)
```

Q33: How to sort dictionary by value?

Ans:
```
import operator as o
countryDict ={'CN': 4, 'FR': 5,`UK`: 1, 'USA': 2, 'IN': 3, 'GM': 6}
print(sorted(countryDict.items(), key=o.itemgetter(1)))
```

Q34: What is the use of shuffle function?

Ans: It is used to arrange the values within the list randomly.

Q35: What is the preferred way to get a value based on key in Python?

Ans: The preferred way to get a value based on key is to use get method with default value.

The default value will be used whenever key is absent in the dictionary.

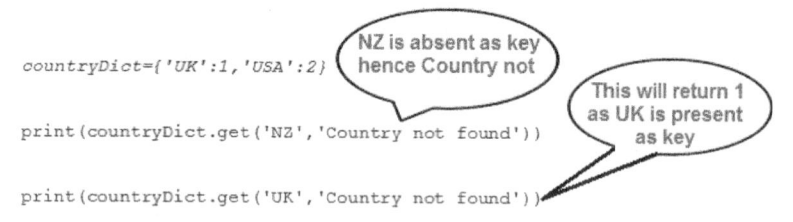

```
countryDict={'UK':1,'USA':2}
```
NZ is absent as key hence Country not

```
print(countryDict.get('NZ','Country not found'))
```
This will return 1 as UK is present as key

```
print(countryDict.get('UK','Country not found'))
```

Q36: Explain alternate way of merging 2 or more dictionaries without using update method?

Ans:
```
countryDict1={'UK':1,'USA':2}

countryDict2={'IN':3,'CN':4}
```
Combines the contents of three dictionaries to generate one final dictionary
```
countryDict3={'FR':5,'GM':6}

countryDict ={**countryDict1,**countryDict2,**countryDict3}

print(countryDict)
```

Q37: **What is the preferred way of fetching last element/second last and so on from a list?**

Ans: Python supports negative indexes on list.
- -1 refers to last element
- -2 refers to second last element
  ```
  l = [1, 2, 3, 4, 5]
  print(l[-1])  #prints 5
  print(l[-2])  #prints 4
  ```

Q38: **What is the preferred way for reversing a list?**

Ans: The preferred way for returning a list is with help of reversed function.

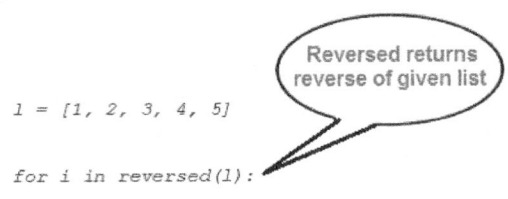

```
l = [1, 2, 3, 4, 5]

for i in reversed(l):

    print (i)
```

Reversed returns reverse of given list

The above code will print the following:
```
5,4,3,2,1
```

Q39: **Explain various string utility functions in Python.**

Ans: **capitalize():** Capitalizes the first letter of string.

isalnum(): Returns true if string has at least 1 character and all characters are alphanumeric and false otherwise.

isdigit(): Returns true if string contains only digits and false otherwise.

islower(): Returns true if string has at least 1 cased character and all cased characters are in lowercase and false otherwise.

isnumeric(): Returns true if a unicode string contains only numeric characters and false otherwise.

isspace(): Returns true if string contains only whitespace characters and false otherwise.

isupper(): Returns true if string has at least one cased character and all cased characters are in uppercase and false otherwise.

lower(): Converts all uppercase letters in string to lowercase.

lstrip(): Removes all leading whitespace in string.

max(str): Returns the max alphabetical character from the string str.

replace(old, new [, max]): Replaces all occurrences of old in string with new or at most max occurrences if max given.

strip([chars]): Performs both lstrip() and rstrip() on string.

swapcase(): Inverts case for all letters in string.

Q40: How to check whether two strings are equal.

Ans: == operator can be used to check whether strings are equal or not.

Q41: Can string use single quote or double quote?

Ans: Both single quote or double quote is allowed but combination of both is not.

Q42: Explain type conversions on collection types.

Ans:

Convert from	Convert to	Syntax
list	Set	B =set([1,2,3])
set	Tuple	B= tuple({5,6,7})
nested list	Dictionary	dict([[1,2],[3,4]])
set	List	list({1,2})

Q43: Explain set theory operations supported by set data type.

Ans:

Operation	Details
isdisjoint	Returns true if both the sets do not have anything in common
A.issubset(B)	Returns true if A is subset of B
B.issuperset(A)	Returns true if B is superset of A
A & B or A.intersection(B)	Returns common elements between A and B
A – B Or A.difference(B)	Returns the difference between A and B

Sample code for above operations:
```
setA = {11,22,33,44,5}
setB = {44,22,1}
setC = {55}
```

```
setD = {44,22,1,447}
print('isdisjoint`,setA.isdisjoint(setC))
print('Is setB subset of setD ',setB.
issubset(setD))
print('Is setD superset of setD ',setD.
issuperset(setB))
print('common elements are ',setA & setB)
print('common elements are ',setA.
intersection(setB))
print('Elements in A but not in B ', setA-
setB)
print('Elements in B but not in A ', setB-
setA)
print('Elements in A but not in B ', setA.
difference(setB))
print('Elements in B but not in A ', setB.
difference(setA))
```
Output:
```
isdisjoint True
Is setB subset of setD True
Is setD superset of setD True
common elements are {44, 22}
common elements are {44, 22}
Elements in A but not in B {33, 11, 5}
Elements in B but not in A {1}
Elements in A but not in B {33, 11, 5}
Elements in B but not in A {1}
```

Q44: Explain frozenset?

Ans: frozenset gives immutability to set i.e. nothing in it can be modified.

Q45: Explain functions in Python?

Ans: A function is a group of statements intended to do particular task. In Python we can define functions with the help of **def**.
```
def fun():
    print('hello`)
```
Above creates a function fun which prints **hello** message.
```
def fun1(ip):
    print('hello`,ip)
```

Above creates a function with the name fun1 which takes parameter ip and prints corresponding hello message with parameters.

```
def area(r):
return 3.14* r * r
```

Above creates a function which returns result with the help of return type.

Q46: What is a Boolean function?

Ans: Boolean function is one which either returns True or False.

```
def isdivisble(num,den):
    if num%den==0:
        return True
    else:
return False
print(isdivisble(10,2))
```

The above functions returns true or false based upon whether the numerator is divisible by denominator.

Q47: Can we specify data type for arguments as well as return types in Python?

Ans: Recent version of Python has support for type annotations which allows doing the same.

Data type of parameters are passed as well as return type mentioned with -> symbol

```
def mul(x: float, y: int) -> float:

    return x * y

print(mul(9,9.9)) # print 89.100000
```

Q48: Explain variable arguments?

Ans: Variable arguments in Python can be achieved with the help of *args.

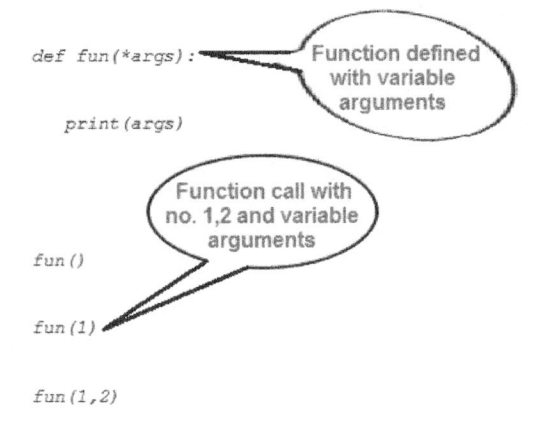

```
def fun(*args):          ← Function defined
                            with variable
    print(args)             arguments

                    Function call with
                    no. 1,2 and variable
fun()                 arguments

fun(1)

fun(1,2)
```

Q49: Write a program to find occurrences or count of characters in given word.

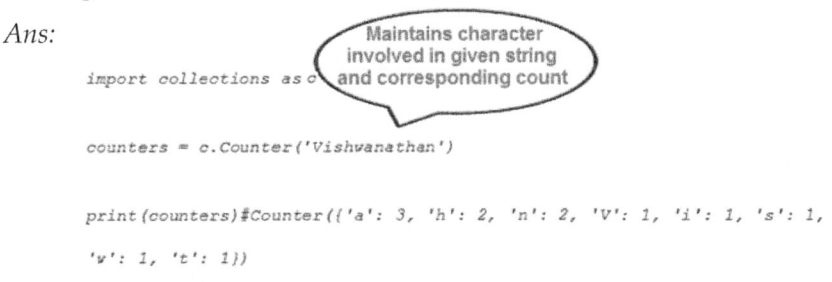

Ans:
```
import collections as c    ← Maintains character
                             involved in given string
                             and corresponding count

counters = c.Counter('Vishwanathan')

print(counters)#Counter({'a': 3, 'h': 2, 'n': 2, 'V': 1, 'i': 1, 's': 1,
'w': 1, 't': 1})
```

Q50: What is **kwargs?

Ans: **kwargs is also variable arguments but in the form of dictionary input also known as keyworded, variable-length argument.

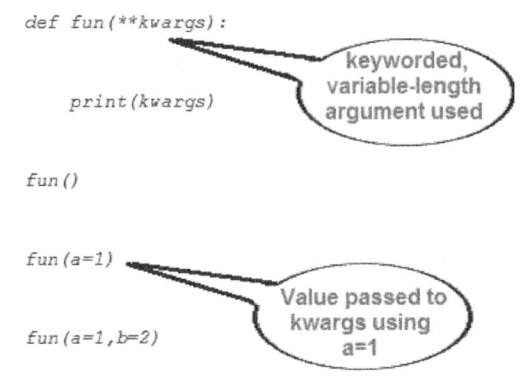

```
def fun(**kwargs):
                          ← keyworded,
                            variable-length
    print(kwargs)           argument used

fun()

fun(a=1)
                     ← Value passed to
                       kwargs using
fun(a=1,b=2)           a=1
```

Q51: Write a simple Lambda expression?

Ans:
```
sumlambda = lambda x, y : x + y
print(sumlambda(2, 3))
```

In the above example, we have defined lambda expression which takes two parameters and performs the addition. The return result is x+ y but no need to return explicitly since it contains single statement only.

Q52: Lambda forms in Python contain statements? True or False?

Ans: Statement is true as lambdas in Python have to be single line expressions.

Q53: Explain filter function?

Ans: The filter function is a utility function which can skip values based on some condition.

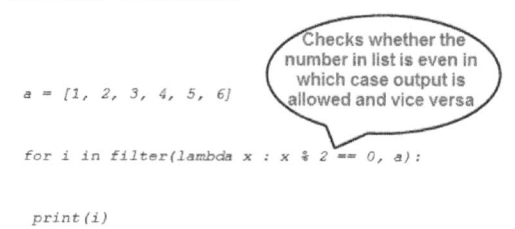

```
a = [1, 2, 3, 4, 5, 6]
```
(Checks whether the number in list is even in which case output is allowed and vice versa)

```
for i in filter(lambda x : x % 2 == 0, a):

    print(i)
```

Q54: Explain steps involved in reading and writing a file?

Ans: In both the case, three steps are involved.

   a. Opening the file.

   b. Reading or writing the file using corresponding functions (read or write).

   3. Closing the file.

Write example:
```
a =open('hello.txt`,`a`) # opens a file in write mode
a.write('welcome to files with python`) # writes this line in file
a.close() # closes the file
```

The above code writes the welcome message to **hello.txt** file.

Read example:
```
a =open('hello.txt`,`r`) # opens a file in read mode
text = a.read() # reads the entire contents of file in memory
print(text) #prints the read text
a.close()# closes the file
```

Q55: Explain the term "withstatement"?

Ans: The **with** statement would be useful whenever there are related operations block on each other.

```
with expression [as variable]:
    with-block
```

In the above statement, we see that **with** block would be used within the context of variable opened with the help of **with** statement.

```
with open('output.txt`, 'w`) as f:
    f.write('|Python!`)
```

In the above example, the file would be closed as soon as the scope of **with** block gets over the advantage of being not to close the file explicitly using close block.

Q56: Explain the preferred way of reading a big file?

Ans:
```
with open("sampleread.txt", "r+") as ip:
    for singleLine in ip:
        print(singleLine)
```

The above code opens the file in read mode with the help of with statement. So, as soon as file operations get over, the file would be automatically closed.

Further the above code loads only a single line in memory at a time thus saving memory or making it possible to run, this program even with computer having lower memory footprint.

Q57: Explain modules in Python.

Ans: Modules both inbuilt and user defined are ways of writing reusable set of code or reusing common set of code.

Python provides set of many inbuilt modules like mathos, sys etc.

To use a module, we will have to import the same with the help of import statement or "from ..import" statement.

Q58: Explain different ways of importing modules.

Ans: Modules can be imported using import statement or *from ..import* statement.

The difference lies in fact whether we want the entire module or particular part of it.

The *from..import* statement is preferred when we want to import particular module.

```
from math import pi
print(pi)
```

The **import** statement is preferred when the entire module is to be imported.

```
import math
print(math.pi)
```

As you can see in import statement we have to use the module name wherever we want to get variables or methods from modules.

Q59: Can we create our own module?

Ans: Yes, we can create our own module. Any Python file itself is a module.

Consider for example following **mathop.py** file containing following code:

```
def sum(a,b):
    return a+b
def sub(a,b):
    return (a-b)
```

In another file named **usage.py** we can write the following code:

```
import mathop
print(mathop.sum(99,100))
print(mathop.sub(99,100))
print(dir(mathop))
```

The above code reads from the modules and performs the required operations.

If the files were in different directory, for example, com folder then we could have imported by giving:

```
com.modulename
```

Q60: Explain in brief about os module and its corresponding functions.

Ans: os module provides various functions to perform operating system related functions especially w.r.t. file operations.

Following are some of the important functions:

os.chdir("D:/pythoneg/intro/pyFolder"): It is used to change the current working directory.

os.mkdir('pyFolder'): It is used to create new directory.

os.remove(): It removes a particular file.

os.getcwd(): It gets the current working directory.

os.environ: It prints environment related details.

os.system(' dir>>1.txt'): It execute a command line related command. For example, executes dir command which is windows command prompt command, to list directories.

os.walk(dir): It lists down sub directory and files within a particular directory.

Q61: Using os module print the directory structure.

Ans:
```
import os
rootDir = 'D:/nodejstraining/NodeJSExample/NodeJSExample`
for dirName, subdirList, fileList in os.walk(rootDir):
    print('Found directory: %s` % dirName)
    for fname in fileList:
print('\t%s` % fname)
```

In the above example we print the directory structure with the help of **os.walk** function which can list down directory name, sub directory list and file list within a particular directory.

Q62: Explain dir function.

Ans: The dir function is used to print various functions which are exposed by a module.

For e.g dir(math) prints all the functions within math module.
```
import math
print(dir(math))
```

Output:
['__doc__`, '__loader__`, '__name__`, '__package__`, '__spec__`, 'acos`, 'acosh`, 'asin`, 'asinh`, 'atan`, 'atan2`, 'atanh`, 'ceil`, 'copysign`, 'cos`, 'cosh`, 'degrees`, 'e`, 'erf`, 'erfc`, 'exp`, 'expm1`, 'fabs`, 'factorial`, 'floor`, 'fmod`, 'frexp`, 'fsum`, 'gamma`, 'gcd`, 'hypot`, 'inf`, 'isclose`, 'isfinite`, 'isinf`, 'isnan`, 'ldexp`, 'lgamma`, 'log`, 'log10`, 'log1p`, 'log2`, 'modf`, 'nan`, 'pi`, 'pow`, 'radians`, 'sin`, 'sinh`, 'sqrt`, 'tan`, 'tanh`, 'tau`, 'trunc`]

Q63: Explain exception handling in Python.

Ans: Exception handling is supported with the help of **try..except** block.

Any statements which can logically cause problems would be placed in **try** block.

In case of exception occurring, corresponding handling is done in except block.

A single try can contain multiple except block.

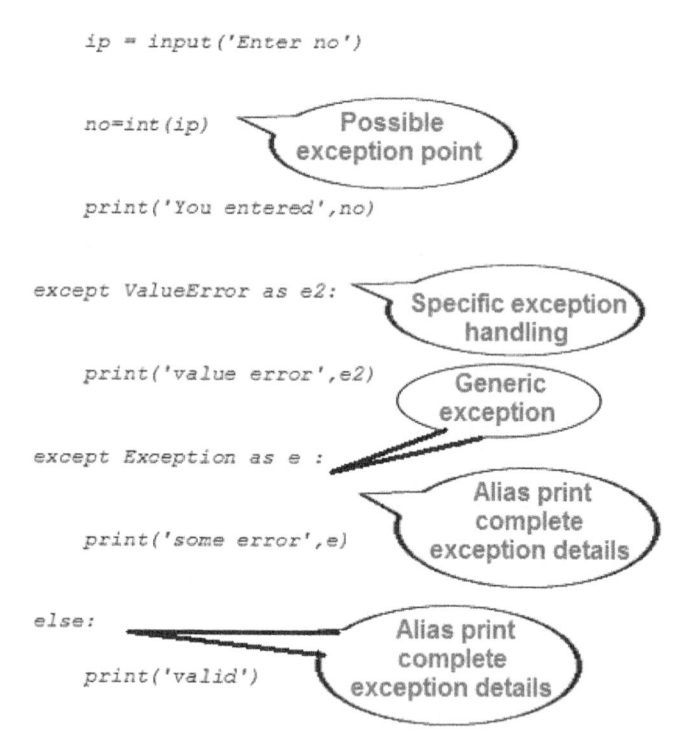

```
try:

    ip = input('Enter no')

    no=int(ip)          ← Possible exception point

    print('You entered',no)

except ValueError as e2:    ← Specific exception handling

    print('value error',e2)     ← Generic exception

except Exception as e :
                              ← Alias print complete exception details
    print('some error',e)

else:                    ← Alias print complete exception details

    print('valid')
```

In the above example, we place the code of accepting input from user and type casting the same to **int** within the try block. We have two except block one catching except block and another generic Exception. Based upon the exception raised, the corresponding except block would be called.

To print the complete details of Exception we make use of alias i.e. *except Exception as e* :makesalias of the exception.

In case of no exception, the else block would be executed.

Q64: How to create user defined exception?

Ans: User defined exceptions are supported in Python.

To create our own exception, we will have to create class with the name of Exception we want, which extends from Exception and correspondingly use it with the help of **raise** statement.

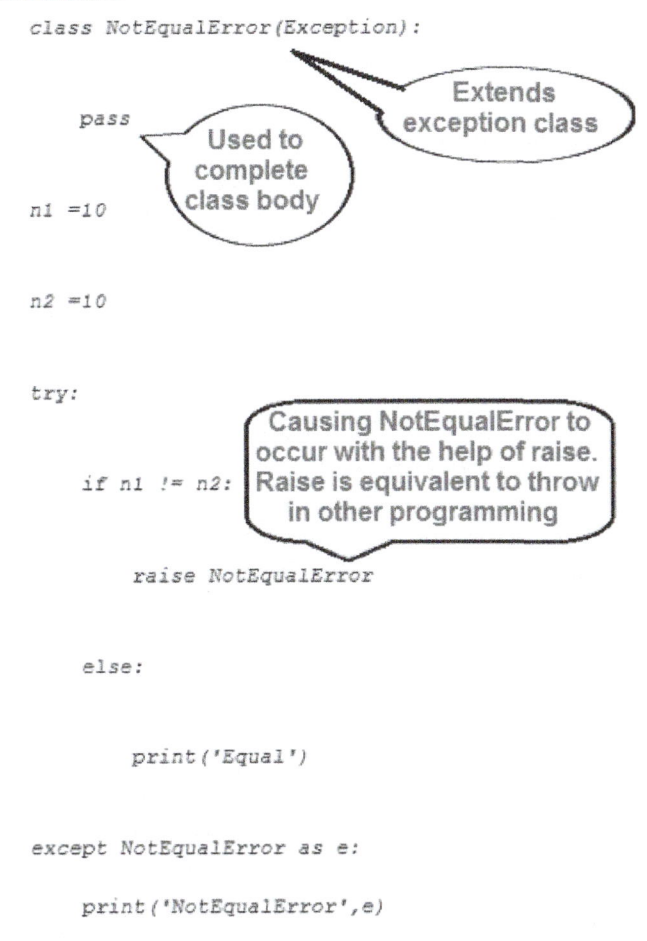

```
class NotEqualError(Exception):
    pass

n1 = 10

n2 = 10

try:
    if n1 != n2:
        raise NotEqualError
    else:
        print('Equal')

except NotEqualError as e:
    print('NotEqualError', e)
```

- `class NotEqualError(Exception):` — Extends exception class
- `pass` — Used to complete class body
- `if n1 != n2: raise NotEqualError` — Causing NotEqualError to occur with the help of raise. Raise is equivalent to throw in other programming

Q65: What is the use of raise statement?

Ans: The **raise** statement is used to generate exception at run time, based upon some condition or constraint imposed.

Q66: How to create own class in Python? Explain constructors.

Ans: We can create our own class in Python. The constructor of the class is specified with the help of **__init__** method.

Any function created as a part of class which is a non-static and non-class method, should have **self** as the first argument which represents the object.

Following is the code to create a class with the name Complex which consists of two members **real** and **img** and one display function.

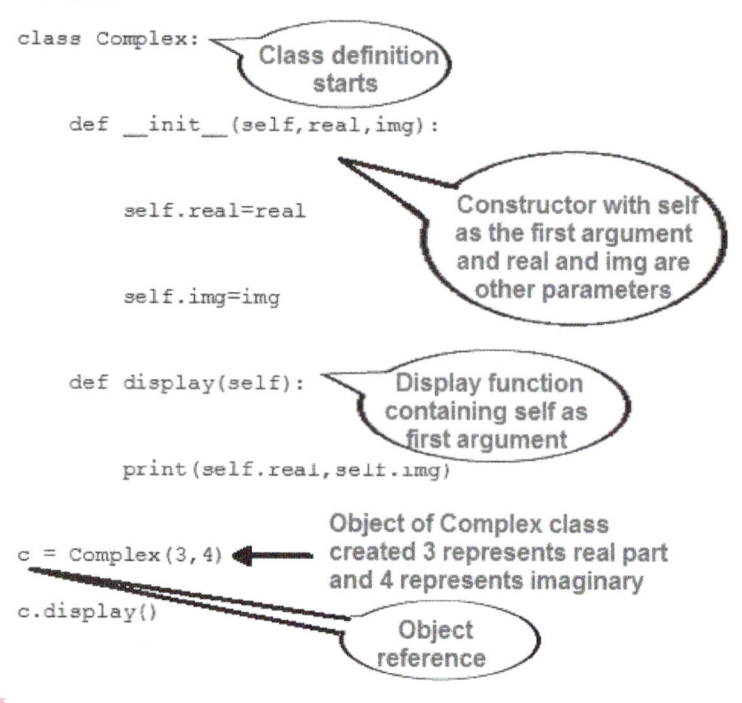

```
class Complex:                    ← Class definition starts
    def __init__(self,real,img):
        self.real=real            ← Constructor with self as the first argument
                                    and real and img are other parameters
        self.img=img

    def display(self):            ← Display function containing self as first argument
        print(self.real,self.img)

c = Complex(3,4)    ← Object of Complex class created 3 represents real part
                      and 4 represents imaginary
c.display()         ← Object reference
```

Q67: Is it necessary to have the first argument of class function as self? Can't we rename it to any other variable?

Ans: The name of the variable can be anything but it always represents the object. The self is the preferred and a general practice naming convention.

Q68: Explain inheritance in Python.

Ans: Python supports inheritance with classes. A class extending another class needs to use ().

Also, super method needs to be used to call base class constructor and methods.

Python Programming Questions ▪ 51

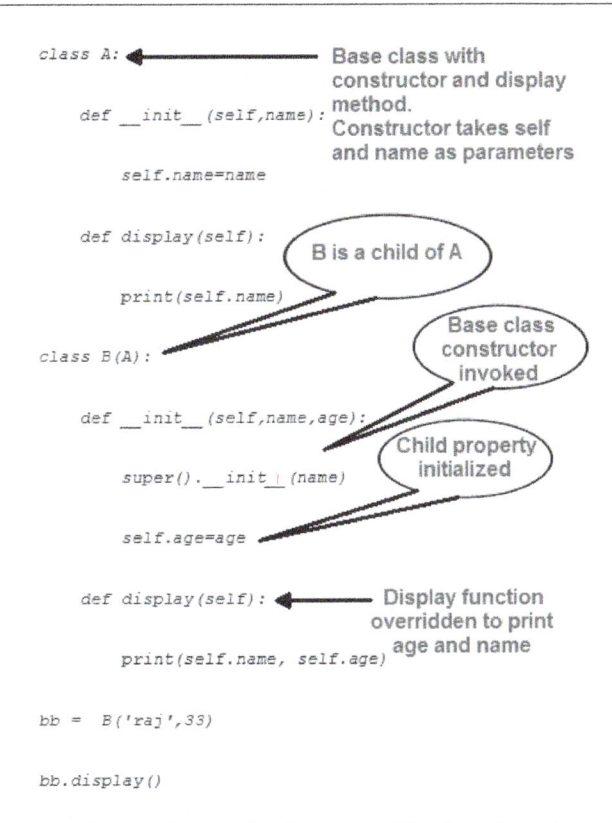

```
class A:                          Base class with
                                  constructor and display
    def __init__(self,name):      method.
                                  Constructor takes self
        self.name=name            and name as parameters

    def display(self):
                                  B is a child of A
        print(self.name)
                                       Base class
class B(A):                            constructor
                                         invoked
    def __init__(self,name,age):
                                     Child property
        super().__init__(name)       initialized

        self.age=age

    def display(self):           Display function
                                 overridden to print
        print(self.name, self.age)  age and name

bb = B('raj',33)

bb.display()
```

Q69: **How to determine whether a particular class is sub class?**
Ans: **issubclass(ChildClass,ParentClass)**

The above function would return true only if the **ChildClass** has inherited from **ParentClass**.

Q70: **Does Python support multiple inheritance?**
Ans: Yes, Python supports multiple inheritance.

A particular class can extend from any number of super classes.

class Child(Parent1,Parent2,......,ParentN):

Q71: **How is diamond problem resolved in case of Python?**
Ans: Diamond problem occurs whenever Child class inherits same method with different body from two different parents.

In the case of Python this is resolved by order in which parent is inherited. Parent which is inherited first is given more importance. In the following example we have two parents both having hello method.

```
class Parent1:

    def hello(self):

        print("Hello from Parent1")

class Parent2:

    def hello(self):

        print("Hello from Parent2")

class Child(Parent1,Parent2):

    pass

c= Child()

c.hello()
```

Parent1 is inherited first

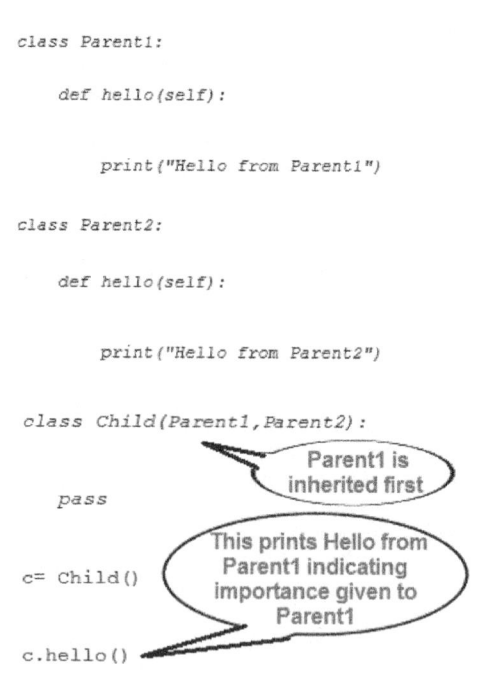

This prints Hello from Parent1 indicating importance given to Parent1

Q72: Does Python support private method and variables?

Ans: Private method and variables are supported in Python. Any variable or method having __ becomes private in nature and cannot be accessed directly by using object.

To get their value we will have to use class name reference from the object.

The main aim of these variables and functions is to ensure that the sub classes do not accidentally override them.

Q73: Can __ be used for other purpose than creating private variables or functions?

Ans: __ has many use cases.

Following are some of them:
  a. Ignoring while assigning values from tuples or list.
     ```
     a, _, b = (11, 220,54)
     ```
     In the above example, a gets value 11 and b gets 54. The __ is used for ignoring the central value 220.
  b. Used to separate numbers *no = 3_200*. This gives better understanding and readability. The number represented here is 3200.

Q74: Does Python support abstract classes?

Ans: Python supports abstract classes with the help of module named **abc**.

An abstract class contains abstract functions and cannot be instantiated.

The abc module contains ABC which stands for Abstract base class and abstract method to do necessary things.

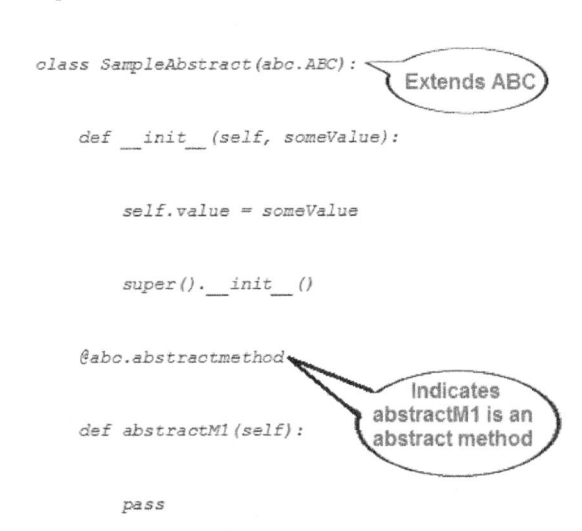

```
import abc

class SampleAbstract(abc.ABC):        ← Extends ABC

    def __init__(self, someValue):

        self.value = someValue

        super().__init__()

    @abc.abstractmethod
                                      Indicates
    def abstractM1(self):             abstractM1 is an
                                      abstract method
        pass
```

The classes which extend the above class have to give body to abstract method else even they cannot be instantiated.

Q75: Differentiate between static methods and class methods in Python.

Ans:

Static method	Class method
Needs no specific parameters though static function can be parameterized.	Takes cls as first parameter. cls represents the class on which the method is created.
Can't modify class state.	Can modify and access class state.
Created by using **@staticmethod** annotation.	Created by using **@classmethod** annotation.
Used to create utilities.	Used to create factories.
No such feature.	Is a descriptor, wrapping a function, and can call the resulting object on a class.
Self-contained code.	Code access till Class level.

Q76: What are named tuple?

Ans: Named tuple allows us to create classes at run time with attributes.

```
from collections import namedtuple

Point = namedtuple('Point', ['x', 'y'])

p1=Point(1, 2)

p2=Point(1,72)

print(p1)

print(p2)
```

Creates a dynamic class with name Point having attributes x and y. First parameter is the name of class and second one is the list of attributes

Q77: How to sort using lamdas?

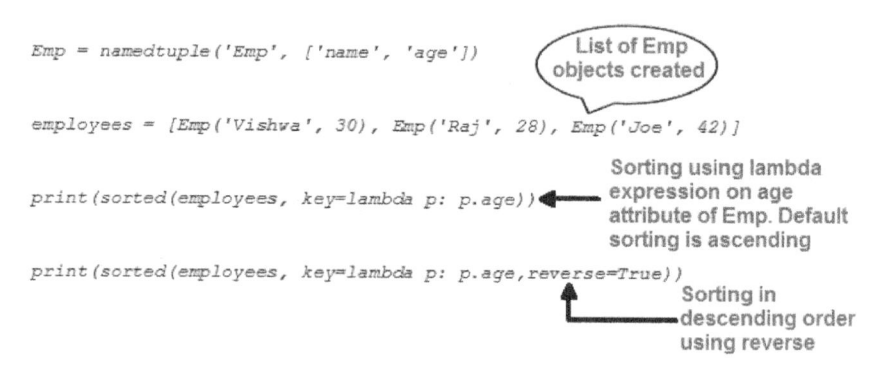

Ans:
```
from collections import namedtuple

Emp = namedtuple('Emp', ['name', 'age'])
```
List of Emp objects created
```
employees = [Emp('Vishwa', 30), Emp('Raj', 28), Emp('Joe', 42)]

print(sorted(employees, key=lambda p: p.age))
```
Sorting using lambda expression on age attribute of Emp. Default sorting is ascending
```
print(sorted(employees, key=lambda p: p.age, reverse=True))
```
Sorting in descending order using reverse

Q78: Explain Generators?

Ans: Generators are used to save memory as they store only some values in memory at a time rather than storing entire dataset in memory.

Generators make use of yield function which stores the previous state to remember.

Generators are invoked using next function.

For example, if we want to process the entire file having million records, generator function would bring only one record at a time in the memory.

```
def fixed_generator(value, max_repeats):

    for i in range(max_repeats):

        yield value      ◄── Generator function
                             makes use of yield

iterator = fixed_generator('Vishwa', 3)

print(next(iterator))
                          ┌─────────────────┐
                          │  Generator is   │
print(next(iterator))     │ called. The value│
                          │ in fixed_generator│
                          │  changes to 0   │
                          └─────────────────┘
print(next(iterator))
```

Q79: What is generator expression?

Ans: The above generators concept can also be applied to expressions.

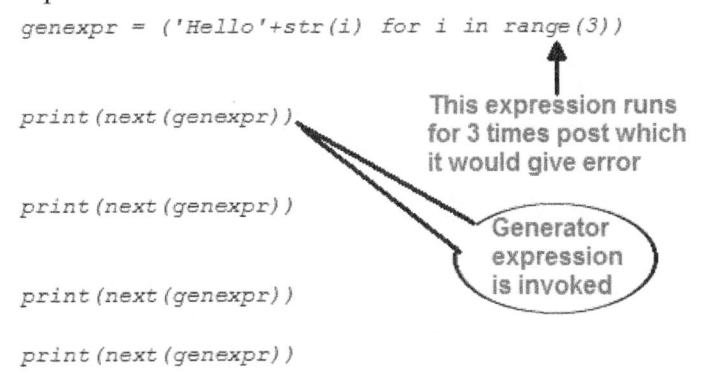

```
genexpr = ('Hello'+str(i) for i in range(3))
                                          ▲
print(next(genexpr))       This expression runs
                           for 3 times post which
                           it would give error
print(next(genexpr))
                          ┌─────────────┐
                          │  Generator  │
print(next(genexpr))      │ expression  │
                          │  is invoked │
                          └─────────────┘
print(next(genexpr))
```

Q80: When Python program exits, all the memory is released? Say true or false?

Ans: **The answer is false because** objects that are referenced from global namespaces of Python modules are not always de-allocated when Python exits.

Q81: Can a function be passed as parameter to another function?

Ans: Yes, it is possible to do the same in Python.

```
def say_hello(a):    ← The parameter a can
                       represent anything
                       including function
    print("Hello from say_hello")

    print("Start Calling function passed")

    a()  ← Parameter passed is
           called as function

    print("Finished Calling function passed")

def say_hi():            ⎛ say_hi is passed ⎞
                         ⎜ as argument to   ⎟
                         ⎝ say_hello        ⎠
    print("Hi from say_hi")

say_hello(say_hi)
```

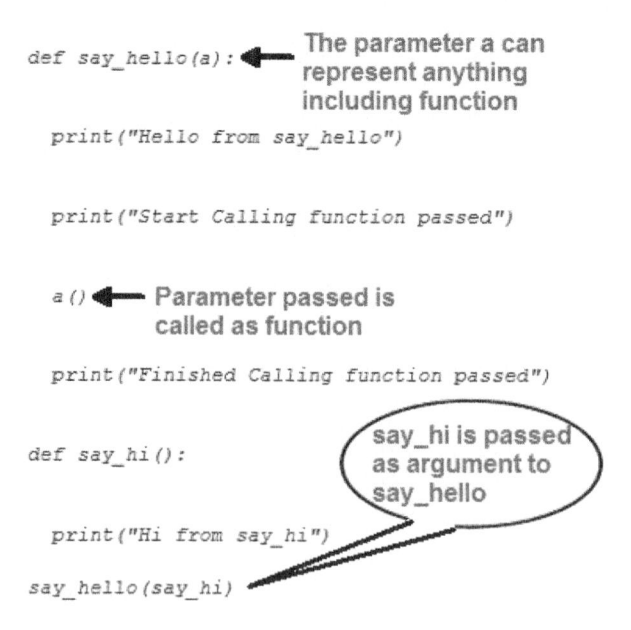

Q82: Can a function be retuned as result from another function?

Ans: Yes, the result of a function can be another function.

```
def say_hello():
                         ⎛ say_hi is the     ⎞
                         ⎜ inner function    ⎟
    print("Hello")       ⎝ within say_hello  ⎠

    def say_hi():
                         ⎛ The say_hi is         ⎞
                         ⎜ retuned as result in  ⎟
        print("Hi")      ⎝ say_hello function    ⎠

    return say_hi
                         The say_hi is
                         retuned as result in
a = say_hello()          say_hello function

                         ⎛ say_hi is ⎞
    print("ddddd")       ⎝ called    ⎠

    a()
```

Q83: Explain decorator function.

Ans: Decorator function allows performing wrapper around a function. It acts as an interceptor which allows performing pre-processing and post-processing.

Python Programming Questions   57

```
                    Decorator function
                    takes another
                    function as argument
def decorator_func(some_func):
                              Inner wrapper function to perform
    def wrapper_func():       pre-processing and post
                              processing before or after calling
                              function passed as argument
        print("Wrapper function started")

        some_func()              Wrapper function is
                                 returned as result
        print("Wrapper function ended")

    return wrapper_func

                          Decorator function
def say_hello():          call which will wrap
                          say_hello function
    print ("Hello")

a = decorator_func(say_hello)

a()
        def decorator_func(a):  ◄─── Same as earlier one

            def wrapper_func(hello_var, world_var):

                return a(hello_var, world_var)

            return wrapper_func      say_hello being annotated with
                                     above created decorator. A
                                     call to say_hello will cause
                                     decorator to be called

        @decorator_func

        def say_hello(hello_var, world_var):

            print(hello_var + " " + world_var)

        say_hello("Welcome ","here")
```

Q84: How can we represent big text in Python?

Ans: Representation of big text is quite simple w.r.t. Python, unlike other programming language.

```
longText = ("Very very very very long text "
            "Very very very very long text "
            "Very very very very long text ")
```

Represented by string within ()

```
print(longText)
```

Q85: What is PEP 8?

Ans: PEP 8 is a coding convention, a set of recommendation, about how to make your Python code more readable. It can be said as globally accepted standards for Python programming.

Q86: What is anaconda?

Ans: Anaconda is easy to use distribution which comes bundled up with lot of modules used in data science world. It provides a packaged environment to get started easily. It also manages dependencies.

Q87: How to install external modules?

Ans: External modules can be easily installed with the help of pip tool which comes bundled with Python.

The command to execute is **python –m pip install module name**.

```
For e.g. python -m pip install numpy
```

In anaconda environment we can install with **conda** command.

```
conda install --name environment_name module
```

Q88: What is Jupyter notebook?

Ans: Jupyter Notebook is a web application that allows you to create and share documents that contain:
- Python code
- visualizations
- explanatory text of code

It can be installed as an external module with the help of **pip**.
```
python -m pip install jupyter
```
Once installed, it can be started by executing command **jupyter notebook**.

The above command will start the web server with notebook opened on web browser.

Notebooks consist of a linear sequence of cells. There are four basic cell types:

- **Code cells:** Input and output of live code that is run in the kernel
- **Markdown cells:** Narrative text with embedded LaTeX equations
- **Heading cells:** 6 levels of hierarchical organization and formatting
- **Raw cells:** Unformatted text that is included

Q89: What is pickling and unpickling?

Ans: Pickling is the process of converting from Python format to intermediate string formats which can be then be stored on file.

Unpickling is the process of bringing or loading the stored Python objects back into memory.

Q90: Explain the importance of setup.py?

Ans: The setup.py allows setting up dependencies easily. While generating one project, it is quite natural to use various libraries. When the same code is shipped to another developer or deployment environment we can make use of setup.py which stores the dependencies on various modules which were used in project.

Q91: Is it possible to make connections to database using Python?

Ans: Python supports connection to database with Db-Api modules.

The mechanism to query remains same but difference lies in the classes to be imported to suit various databases.

To connect to database (in our case MYSQ L) we use the following code:

```
import mysql.connector
```
Connector for Mysql. Similarly different connectors exist for different databases

```
mydb = mysql.connector.connect(
   host="localhost",
   port=3306,
   user="root",
   passwd="root",
   database='pymsql'
)
```
Details of database including username, password, ip address of server, port and schema name

To fetch data from database table:

```
mycursor = mydb.cursor()
```
Create a cursor to execute query

```
sql = "SELECT * FROM vishwa ORDER BY name DESC"

mycursor.execute(sql)
```
SQL is executed here

```
myresult = mycursor.fetchall()

for x in myresult:
```
Results of query is fetched here and stored in myresult variable

```
   print(x)
```
Looping through resultset to print data row by row or tuple by tuple

Delete example:

```
mycursor = mydb.cursor()

sql = "DELETE FROM vishwa WHERE address = 'Chembur"

mycursor.execute(sql)
mydb.commit()
```
Commit to finally commit the transaction in database

Insert example:

Insert can be done using **execute** or **executemany**. Difference lies in fact that execute just takes one record while **executemany** takes many records.

```
sql = "INSERT INTO vishwa (name, address) VALUES (%s, %s)"

val = [

    ('Vishwa',' Chembur'),

    ('Shiv', 'Mulund')

]

mycursor.executemany(sql, val)          ← Execute many to insert more than one records in database

mydb.commit()
```

Update example:

```
sql = "UPDATE vishwa SET address = %s WHERE name = %s"

val = ("Mulund", "Vishwa")

mycursor.execute(sql, val)              ← Parameters passed as positions the values of which are set in execute query
```

Q92: **Explain meta programming?**

Ans: This is a programming technique in which program itself is treated as data. Such languages do have knowledge of itself, and can change or manipulate itself during run time.

Following are some of the examples of meta programming in Python:

a. Adding attribute and method to class.

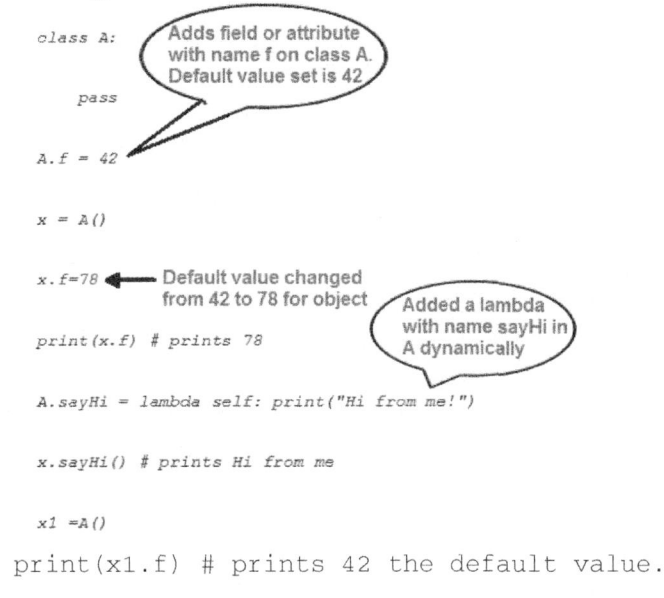

```
class A:                    ← Adds field or attribute with name f on class A. Default value set is 42
    pass

A.f = 42

x = A()

x.f=78   ← Default value changed from 42 to 78 for object

print(x.f)  # prints 78     ← Added a lambda with name sayHi in A dynamically

A.sayHi = lambda self: print("Hi from me!")

x.sayHi()  # prints Hi from me

x1 =A()

print(x1.f) # prints 42 the default value.
```

b. Creating inheritance chain using type.

The type method can not only be used to get the type of variable but can also be used for meta programming. Details of overloaded type, is as follows:

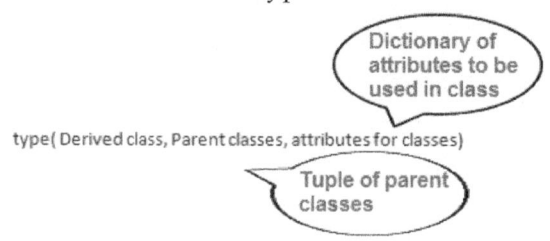

type(Derived class, Parent classes, attributes for classes)

- Dictionary of attributes to be used in class
- Tuple of parent classes

For example:
```
B = type(B, (A,), dict(f=100))
```
The above statement creates class B which inherits from Class A and has field f with value 100.

c. Creating dynamic constructor or linking constructor.

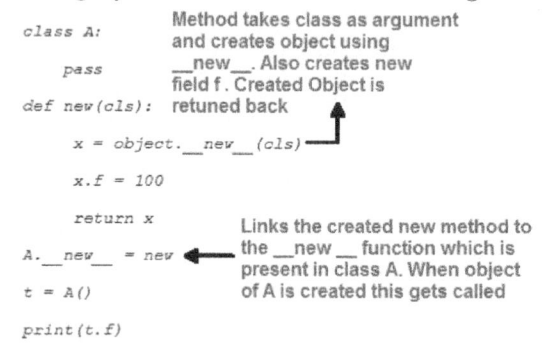

```
class A:
    pass
    def new(cls):
        x = object.__new__(cls)
        x.f = 100
        return x
A.__new__ = new
t = A()
print(t.f)
```

Method takes class as argument and creates object using __new__. Also creates new field f. Created Object is retuned back

Links the created new method to the __new__ function which is present in class A. When object of A is created this gets called

d. Complete meta class example:

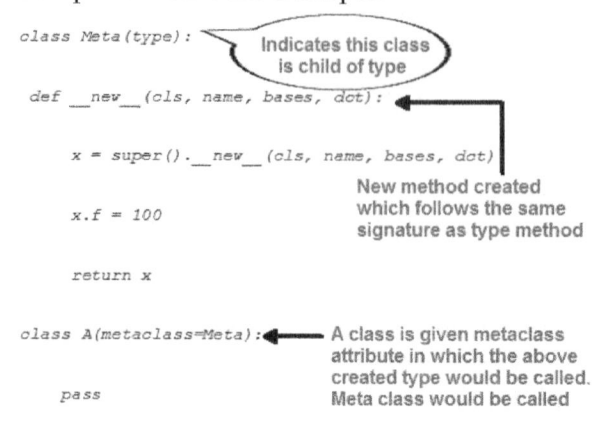

```
class Meta(type):
    def __new__(cls, name, bases, dct):
        x = super().__new__(cls, name, bases, dct)
        x.f = 100
        return x

class A(metaclass=Meta):
    pass

print(A.f) ## prints 100 set up in Meta class
```

Indicates this class is child of type

New method created which follows the same signature as type method

A class is given metaclass attribute in which the above created type would be called. Meta class would be called

Q93: Explain Python memory model.

Ans:

```
   Allocation of              Periodically clean
     Memory                   memory variables
   happens here               which are not used
        ↓                            ↓
   ┌──────────────┐          ┌──────────────────┐
   │Python Memory │          │ Garbage Collector│
   │   Manager    │          │                  │
   └──────────────┘          └──────────────────┘
   ┌────────────────────────────────┐      Data Structures
   │    Heap Space of Memory        │ ←──  and Objects are
   └────────────────────────────────┘      stored here
```

CHAPTER 3
Numpy Interview Questions

Note: [Q: Question Number and Ans: Answer]

Q1: What is numpy?

Ans: The **numpy** is a module which is responsible for effectively storing and processing the same at a faster rate as compared to normal array. The advantage of **numpy** is support of large number of in built mathematical operations as compared to other programming language. Also, the support to represent n dimensions is also possible with **numpy**.

Q2: How to install numpy?

Ans: Since **numpy** is an external module it can be installed using **pip**.

```
python -m pip install numpy
```

Q3: How to create single dimension numpy array?

Ans:
```
import numpy as np          # Imports numpy and aliases it as np
ip = [1, 2.5, 8, 0, 1]
arr1 = np.array(ip)         # Creates numpy array from list
print(arr1)   #prints [1.  2.5 8.  0.  1. ]
```

Q4: Explain different attributes provided by numpy?

Ans: numpy provides the following attributes:

ndim: As **numpy** provides **n** dimensions, we can get how many dimensions currently the array is having with **ndim**.

shape: Indicates number of rows and columns which again can be in different dimensions.

dtype: Indicates data type of elements stored in **numpy**.

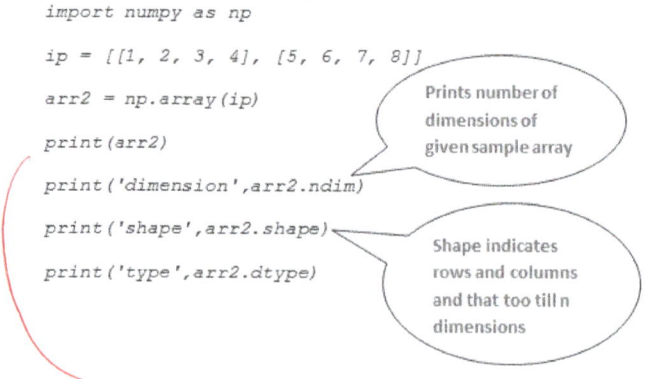

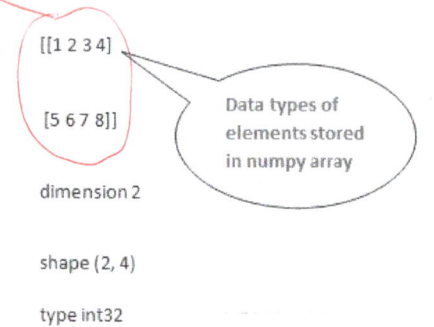

```
import numpy as np
ip = [[1, 2, 3, 4], [5, 6, 7, 8]]
arr2 = np.array(ip)
print(arr2)
print('dimension', arr2.ndim)
print('shape', arr2.shape)
print('type', arr2.dtype)
```

Prints number of dimensions of given sample array

Shape indicates rows and columns and that too till n dimensions

Output:

[[1 2 3 4]

[5 6 7 8]]

Data types of elements stored in numpy array

dimension 2

shape (2, 4)

type int32

Q5: Explain some utility methods provided by numpy for creating different elements?

Ans: np.zeros(length) creates a numpy array at all zeroes occupying the length specified. Can also take rows and columns and create **n** dimensions filled with zeroes.

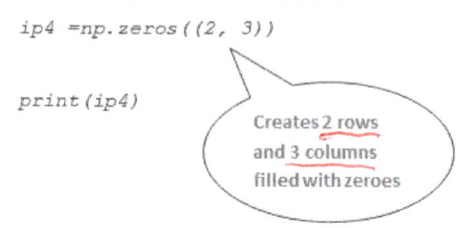

```
ip4 = np.zeros((2, 3))
print(ip4)
```

Creates 2 rows and 3 columns filled with zeroes

Output:
```
[[0. 0. 0.]
 [0. 0. 0.]
```
np.ones: Can create either single dimension or **n** dimension, all filled with ones.
```
ip4 =np.ones((2, 3))
print(ip4)
```
Output:
```
[[1. 1. 1.]
 [1. 1. 1.]]
```
np.eye: Creates a representation in which diagonal elements are zeroes.
```
ip8 =np.eye(3,3)
print(ip8)
```
Output:
```
[[1. 0. 0.]
 [0. 1. 0.]
 [0. 0. 1.]]
```
np.arange: Create a single or **n** dimension array in which numbers are populated starting from 0 to the number specified as parameter.
```
ip6=np.arange((5))
print(ip6)
```
Output:
```
[0 1 2 3 4]
```

Q6: **How can we change shape of an object?**

Ans: Shape of the object can be changed with shape attribute or reshape method.

Shape attribute:
```
import numpy as np

a = np.array([[1,2,3],[4,5,6]])

print('shape',a.shape)        ← Will give shape as (2, 3)

print('before',a)

a.shape = (3,2)               ← Changing the shape from 2,3 to 3,2

print('after change',a)
```

Output:
```
shape (2, 3)
```
Before,
```
[[1 2 3]
 [4 5 6]]
```
After change,
```
[[1 2]
 [3 4]
 [5 6]]
```

reshape:

Allows the dimensions to be specified based on which, the shape can be changed.
```
a = np.array([[1,2,3],[4,5,6]])
b = a.reshape(3,2)
print('reshape`, b)
```

Output:
```
[[1 2]
 [3 4]
 [5 6]]
```

Q7: **Which all data types are supported in Python?**

Ans: int8, uint8 i1, u1 int16, uint16 i2, u2 int32, uint32 i4, u4 int64, uint64 : Signed and unsigned 8-bit (1 byte) 16-bit integer types or 32-bit or 64-bit integer types

float16 float32 float64, float128 Floating point with 16.32,64 or 128 bits

complex64, complex128, complex256 Complex numbers represented by two 32, 64, or 128

bool ?: Boolean type storing True and False values

object O : Python object type

string_ S : Fixed-length string type (1 byte per character)

unicode_U : Fixed-length unicode type (platform specific number of bytes)

Q8: **Explain various simple mathematical operations which can be done on numpy?**

Ans:

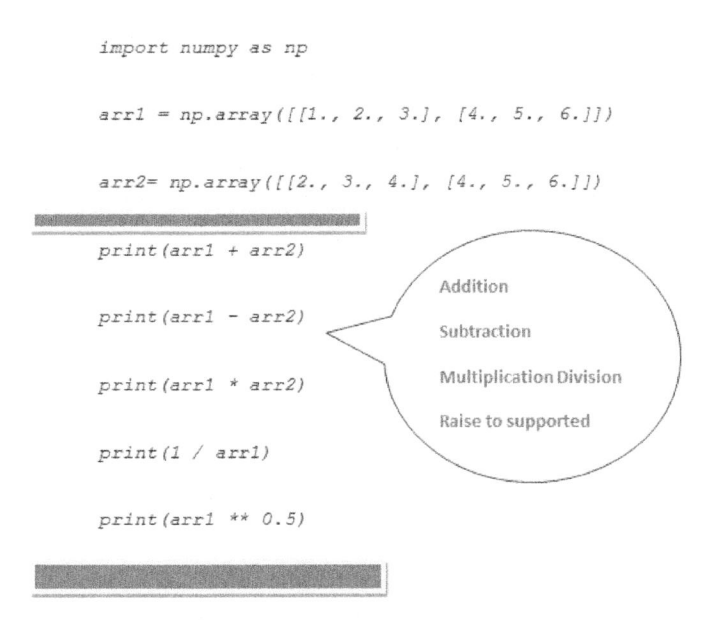

```
import numpy as np

arr1 = np.array([[1., 2., 3.], [4., 5., 6.]])

arr2= np.array([[2., 3., 4.], [4., 5., 6.]])

print(arr1 + arr2)

print(arr1 - arr2)

print(arr1 * arr2)

print(1 / arr1)

print(arr1 ** 0.5)
```

Addition
Subtraction
Multiplication Division
Raise to supported

Q9: Explain slicing operation in numpy?

Ans: Slicing means getting data from **numpy** array via row or columns or both.

General slicing on single dimension [start:end].

Start element is inclusive end element is exclusive.

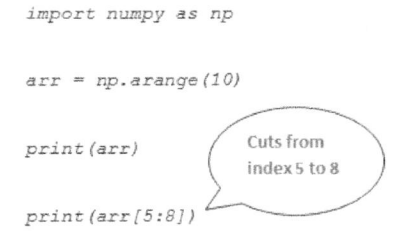

```
import numpy as np

arr = np.arange(10)

print(arr)

print(arr[5:8])
```

Cuts from index 5 to 8

Output:

[5 6 7]

For 2 dimensions and more than 2 dimensions, we can specify slicing by row and column indexes. In such case, following is the slicing.

[rowStart:rowEnd,columnStart:columnEnd]

- If **rowStart** is not specified, starts from zero
- If **rowEnd** is not specified, goes all the way till end
- If **columnStart** not specified, starts from zero
- If **columnEnd** not specified, goes till end

For example:

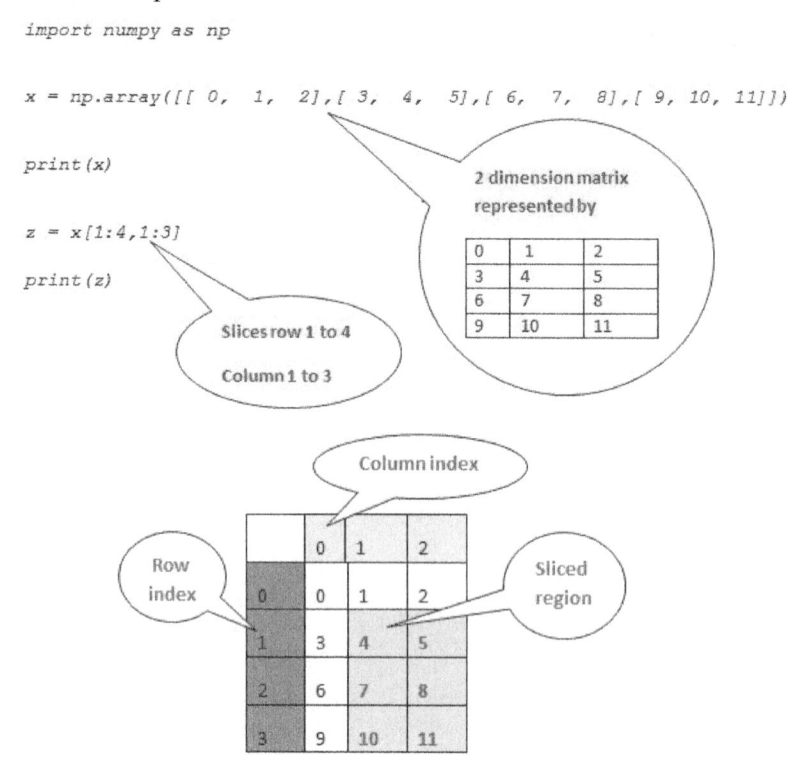

```
import numpy as np

x = np.array([[ 0,  1,  2],[ 3,  4,  5],[ 6,  7,  8],[ 9, 10, 11]])

print(x)

z = x[1:4,1:3]

print(z)
```

2 dimension matrix represented by

0	1	2
3	4	5
6	7	8
9	10	11

Slices row 1 to 4 Column 1 to 3

Column index

	0	1	2
0	0	1	2
1	3	4	5
2	6	7	8
3	9	10	11

Row index — Sliced region

Q10: Explain Boolean indexing?

Ans: Boolean indexing return True or False based on some condition.

Consider the following numpy array with names.

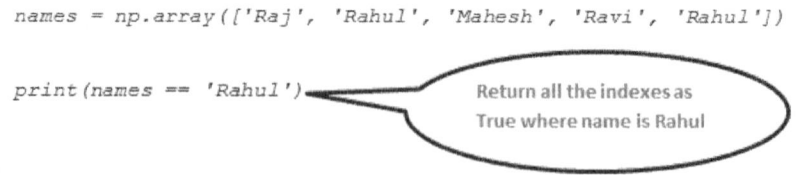

```
names = np.array(['Raj', 'Rahul', 'Mahesh', 'Ravi', 'Rahul'])

print(names == 'Rahul')
```

Return all the indexes as True where name is Rahul

Output:

[False True False False True]

Raj	Rahul	Mahesh	Ravi	Rahul
False	True	False	False	True

Boolean Indexing can also be masked that is, it can have more than one condition.

(names == 'Rahul`) | (names == 'Raj`)

The above code returns true for both Rahul and Raj.

Q11: Perform matrix multiplication using numpy?

Ans: Matrix multiplication can be easily achieved with the help of dot function.

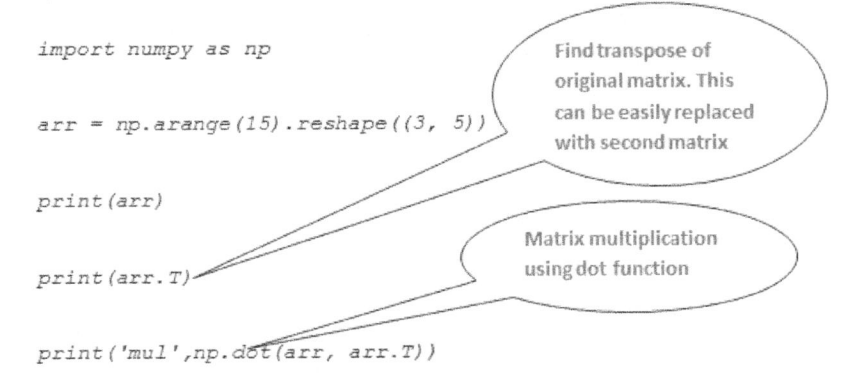

```
import numpy as np

arr = np.arange(15).reshape((3, 5))

print(arr)

print(arr.T)

print('mul',np.dot(arr, arr.T))
```

Find transpose of original matrix. This can be easily replaced with second matrix

Matrix multiplication using dot function

Q12: Explain various functions available with numpy?

Ans: **numpy** supports the following function. The advantage of given functions are that they are applied on all the elements of **numpy** array.

abs, fabs: Returns the absolute value element-wise for .
Fabs can be used for non-complex-valued data with additional speed.

sqrt: Square root of each element is calculated.

squar e: Square of each element is calculated.

exp: Exponent ex of each element is calculated.

log: log10, log2, log1p Natural logarithm (base e), log base 10, log base 2, and log(1 + x), respectively.

sign: sign of each element: 1 (positive), 0 (zero), or -1 (negative) is calculated.

ceil: Determines the ceiling of each element,

floor: Determines the floor of each element,

rint: Round elements to the nearest integer, preserving the dtype.

modf: Return fractional and integral parts of given input

isnan: Returns true if the value is NaN else false

isfinite, isinf: Return true indicating whether each element is finite or infinite, respectively.

Regular and hyperbolic trigonometric functions

cos, cosh, sin, sinh,tan, tanh ,arccos, arccosh, arcsin,arcsinh, arctan, arctanh

maximum, fmax Element-wise maximum. fmax ignores NaN
minimum, fmin Element-wise minimum. fmin ignores NaN
mod Element-wise modulus (remainder of division)
copysign Copy sign of values in second argument to values in first argument

Q13: What is broadcast?

Ans: The ability of **numpy** to treat arrays with different dimensions or shape in a uniform way is known as broadcasting.

We can do broadcasting with the help of broadcast method.

```
import numpy as np

x = np.array([[1], [2], [3]])

y = np.array([4, 5, 6])

b = np.broadcast(y,x)

for t in b:
    print(t)
```

Will repeat each element of y w.r.t x for example 4 will be repeated with all elements of x and so on

Output:
(4, 1)
(5, 1)
(6, 1)
(4, 2)
(5, 2)
(6, 2)
(4, 3)
(5, 3)
(6, 3)

Q14: Explain rules of broadcasting.

- Whenever two arrays have different dimensions the shape of the one with fewer dimensions is adjusted by padding with ones on its leading (left) side.
- If there is a difference in the shape of the two arrays, it does not match in any dimension, then dimension is stretched to match the other shape for that array with shape one.
- An error is raised in case the dimension and sizes disagree, and neither is equal to 1.

Numpy Interview Questions — 73

Q15: **Explain some statistical measures supported by numpy.**

Ans: **amin:** Find the minimum value row wise or column wise

mean: Finds the mean value of given dataset

std: Finds standard deviation of given dataset

var: Finds variance of given dataset

average: Finds weighted average in which average is calculated based upon frequency of occurrence of variables

percentile: Calculates various percentile intervals mostly around 25, 50 and 75%

ptp: Calculates peak to peak values in a given dataset

median: Calculates median from given dataset

```
import numpy as np

a = np.array([[3,7,5],[8,4,3],[2,4,9]])

print('a')

print(a)                    # 1 indicates calculates based on row

print('amin 1')

print (np.amin(a,1) )       # 0 indicates calculate based on column

print('amin 0')

print (np.amin(a,0) )

print('ptp')

print (np.ptp(a) )

print('ptp axis 0')
print (np.ptp(a, axis = 0) )
print('percentile axis 1')
print (np.percentile(a,50, axis = 1) )
print('percentile axis 0')
print (np.percentile(a,50, axis = 0) )
print('median')
```

```
print (np.median(a, axis = 0) )
print('mean`)
print (np.mean(a, axis = 0) )
a = np.array([1,2,3,4])
wts = np.array([4,3,2,1])
print('average`)
print (np.average(a,weights = wts) )
print('std`)
print (np.std([1,2,3,4]))
print('var`)
print (np.var([1,2,3,4]))
```

Output:
```
a
   [[3 7 5]
   [8 4 3]
   [2 4 9]]
amin 1
[3 3 2]
amin 0
[2 4 3]
ptp
7
ptp axis 0
[6 3 6]
percentile axis 1
[5. 4. 4.]
percentile axis 0
[3. 4. 5.]
median
[3. 4. 5.]
mean
[4.33333333 5.      5.66666667]
average
2.0
std
1.118033988749895
var
1.25
```

Q16: Explain functions available in numpy.linalg.

Ans: **dot(a, b[, out]):** Dot product of two arrays.

linalg.multi_dot(arrays): Compute the dot product of two or more arrays in a single function call, while automatically selecting the fastest evaluation order.

vdot(a, b): Return the dot product of two vectors.

inner(a, b): Inner product of two arrays.

outer(a, b[, out]): Compute the outer product of two vectors.

matmul(a, b[, out]): Matrix product of two arrays.

tensordot(a, b[, axes]): Compute tensor dot product along specified axes for arrays >= 1-D.

einsum(subscripts, *operands[, out, dtype, ...]): Evaluates the Einstein summation convention on the operands.

linalg.matrix_power(M, n): Raise a square matrix to the (integer) power **n**.

kron(a, b): Kronecker product of two arrays.

linalg.cholesky(a): Cholesky decomposition.

linalg.qr(a[, mode]): Compute the qr factorization of a matrix.

linalg.svd(a[, full_matrices, compute_uv]): Singular Value Decomposition.

Matrix eigenvalues linalg.eig(a): Compute the eigenvalues and right eigenvectors of a square array.

linalg.eigh(a[, UPLO]): Return the eigenvalues and eigenvectors of a Hermitian or symmetric matrix.

linalg.eigvals(a): Compute the eigenvalues of a general matrix.

linalg.eigvalsh(a[, UPLO]): Compute the eigenvalues of a Hermitian or real symmetric matrix.

linalg.norm(x[, ord, axis, keepdims]): Matrix or vector norm.

linalg.cond(x[, p]): Compute the condition number of a matrix.

linalg.det(a): Compute the determinant of an array.

linalg.matrix_rank(M[, tol]): Return matrix rank of array using SVD method.

linalg.slogdet(a): Compute the sign and (natural) logarithm of the determinant of an array.

trace(a[, offset, axis1, axis2, dtype, out]): Return the sum along diagonals of the array.

linalg.solve(a, b): Solve a linear matrix equation, or system of linear scalar equations.

linalg.tensorsolve(a, b[, axes]): Solve the tensor equation a x = b for x.

linalg.lstsq(a, b[, rcond]): Return the least-squares solution to a linear matrix equation.

linalg.inv(a): Compute the (multiplicative) inverse of a matrix.

linalg.pinv(a[, rcond]): Compute the (Moore-Penrose) pseudo-inverse of a matrix.

linalg.tensorinv(a[, ind]): Compute the 'inverse' of an N-dimensional array.

Q17: How to save numpy data from memory to flat file?

Ans: numpy data can be stored in **npy** format files which are custom serialized or they can be stored in text file.

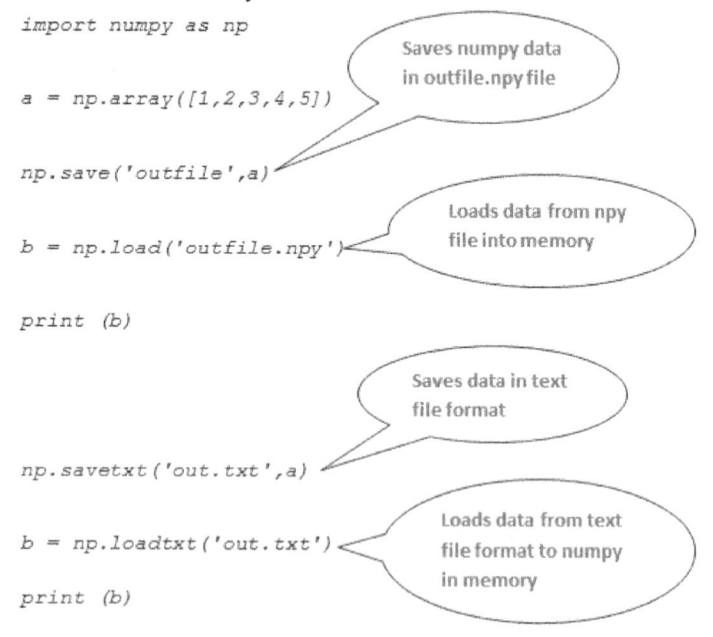

```
import numpy as np

a = np.array([1,2,3,4,5])

np.save('outfile',a)          # Saves numpy data in outfile.npy file

b = np.load('outfile.npy')    # Loads data from npy file into memory

print (b)

np.savetxt('out.txt',a)       # Saves data in text file format

b = np.loadtxt('out.txt')     # Loads data from text file format to numpy in memory

print (b)
```

Q18: What is the use of where and extract?

Ans: Both **where** and **extract** are used to match data based on the conditions.

Where sample:

```
import numpy as np

x = np.arange(9.).reshape(3, 3)

print(x)
```

> Finds out the index where value is greater than 3

```
y = np.where(x > 3)

print (x[y])
```

> Prints the value corresponding to condition
> [4. 5. 6. 7. 8.]

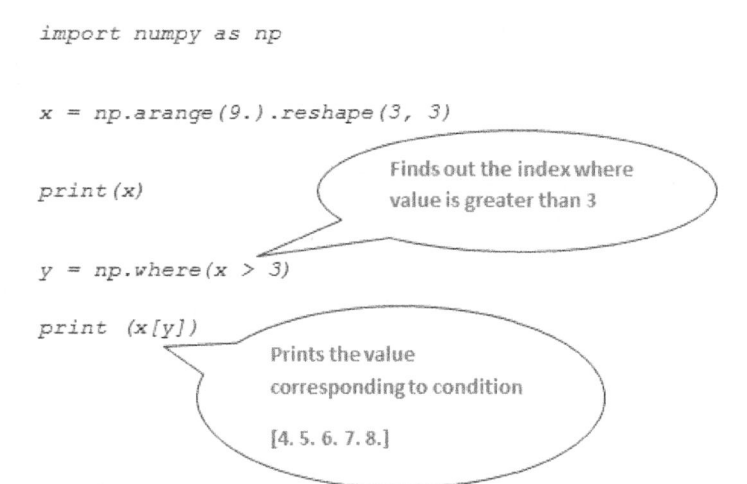

Extract: Specifies data and corresponding condition.

```
x = np.arange(9.).reshape(3, 3)

condition = np.mod(x,2) == 0
```

> Applies above created condition on dataset

```
print( condition )

print (np.extract(condition, x))
```

Q19: What is the use of ndenumerate?

Ans: **ndenumerate** return the co-ordinates and corresponding values in the co-ordinates.

```
A = np.array([[11, 22], [33, 43]])
    for index, x in np.ndenumerate(a):
        print(index, x)
```

Output:
```
(0, 0) 11
(0, 1) 22
(1, 0) 33
(1, 1) 43
```

Q20: Explain how can we draw a histogram using numpy?

Ans: Consider the following code:

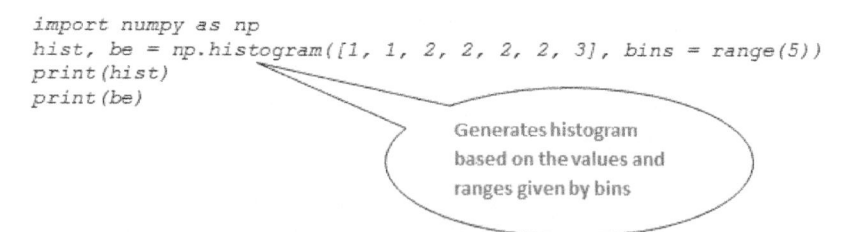

```
import numpy as np
hist, be = np.histogram([1, 1, 2, 2, 2, 2, 3], bins = range(5))
print(hist)
print(be)
```

Generates histogram based on the values and ranges given by bins

The output given will be as follows:

Range	Bin	Count
0-1	0	1
1-2	1	2
2-3	2	4
3-4	3	1

The print(be) method in the above prints bin while the hist prints the corresponding count.

CHAPTER 4
Pandas Interview Questions

Note: [Q: Question Number and Ans: Answer]

Q1: What is Pandas?

Ans: Pandas is a third party module which helps in easier representation of data in memory to perform analysis. Pandas help in faster representation and processing of data.

Q2: How does Pandas represent data?

Ans: Pandas data representation is in similar line to an excel sheet which consists of row and columns.

Columns in Pandas are known as series.

Collection of series is called data frame.

Thus, data frame is the unit of representation of data which is collection of various series.

Shown is the representation of data frame:

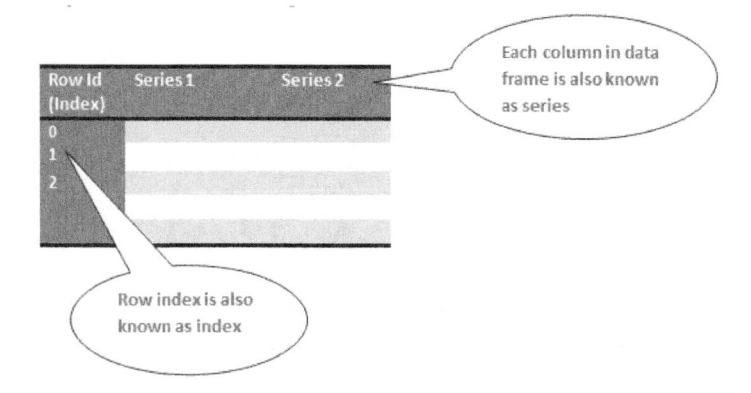

Each column in data frame is also known as series

Row index is also known as index

Q3: How to create Series?

Ans:

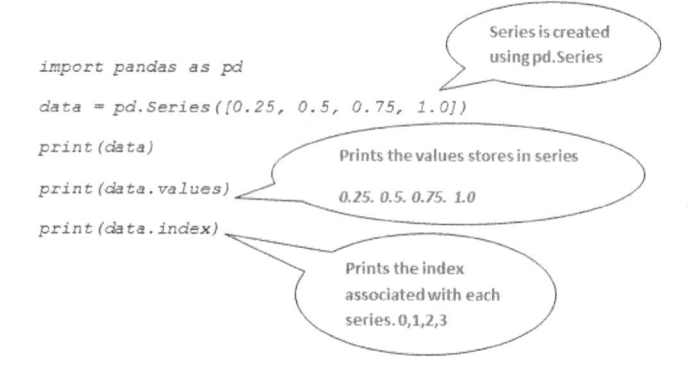

```
import pandas as pd
data = pd.Series([0.25, 0.5, 0.75, 1.0])
print(data)
print(data.values)
print(data.index)
```

Series is created using pd.Series

Prints the values stores in series
0.25. 0.5. 0.75. 1.0

Prints the index associated with each series. 0,1,2,3

Q4: How to create Data frame?

Ans: Data frame can be created directly from dictionary or it can also be created by combining various series.

```
import pandas as pd
country_population =
{'India': 1100000,
'China': 45679000,
'USA': 3400000}
population = pd.Series(country_population)
country_land = {'India': '20000 hectares',
'China': '40000 hectares',
'USA': '30000 hectares'}
area = pd.Series(country_land)
df = pd.DataFrame({'Population': population,'SpaceOccupied': area})
print(df)
```

Creates a population series from country_population dictionary

Creates an area series from country_land

Data frame created with this two series

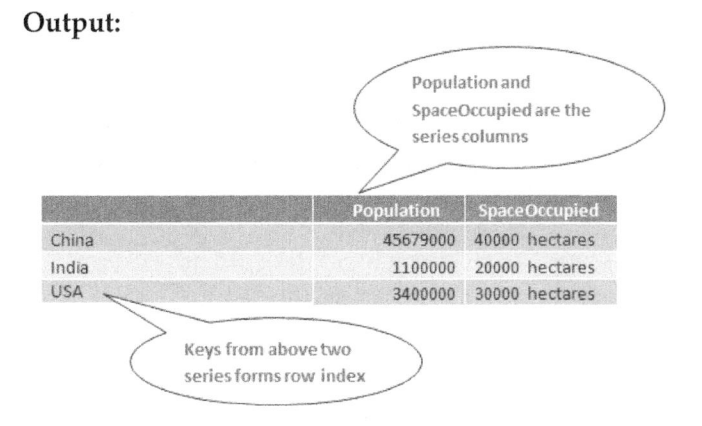

Output:

Population and SpaceOccupied are the series columns

	Population	SpaceOccupied
China	45679000	40000 hectares
India	1100000	20000 hectares
USA	3400000	30000 hectares

Keys from above two series forms row index

Q5: How are missing values represented in data frame?

Ans: Consider the following example:

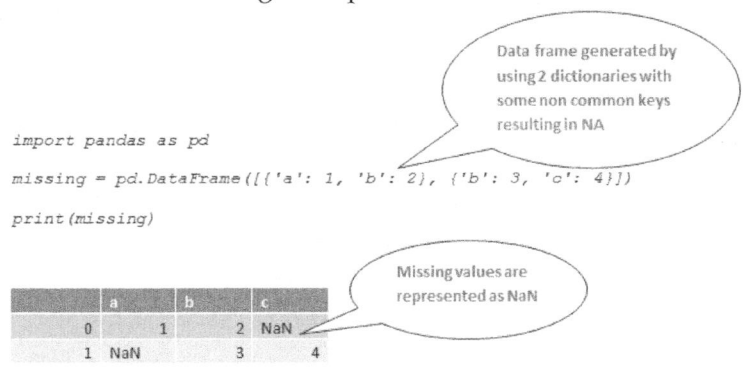

Data frame generated by using 2 dictionaries with some non common keys resulting in NA

```
import pandas as pd
missing = pd.DataFrame([{'a': 1, 'b': 2}, {'b': 3, 'c': 4}])
print(missing)
```

	a	b	c
0	1	2	NaN
1	NaN	3	4

Missing values are represented as NaN

Q6: Explain the process of creating indexes w.r.t. pandas?

Ans: Indexes can be created using pd.Index function. Indexes support intersection and union.

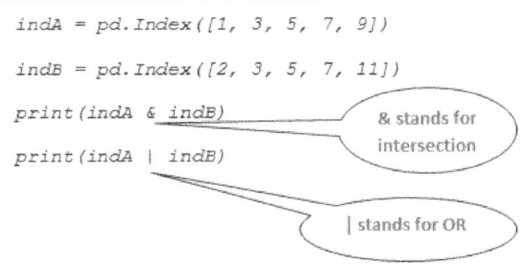

```
indA = pd.Index([1, 3, 5, 7, 9])
indB = pd.Index([2, 3, 5, 7, 11])
print(indA & indB)
print(indA | indB)
```

& stands for intersection

| stands for OR

Q7: Explain various attributes associated with series.

Ans: **axes:** Stands for row.

dtype: The data type of the object is given by this attribute.

empty: Checks if series is empty.

ndim: The dimensions of data are given back.

size: Size or number of elements from data are given.

values: Gets the values in the form of ndarray.

head(): The first n rows are returned.

tail(): The last n rows are returned.

```
import pandas as pd
import numpy as np
s = pd.Series(np.random.randn(4))
print('series`,s)
print('axes`,s.axes)
print('Empty`,s.empty)
print("Dimensions:")
print(s.ndim)
print ("Size of the object:")
print (s.size)
print ("Underlying data is:")
print (s.values)
print ("Top 2 rows:")
print (s.head(2))
print ("Last 2 rows:")
print (s.tail(2))
```

Output:
```
eries 0  -0.200094
1       0.923716
2       -0.565540
3       -0.895206
dtype: float64
axes [RangeIndex(start=0, stop=4, step=1)]
Empty False
Dimensions:
1
Size of the object:
4
Underlying data is:
[-0.20009423  0.92371595  -0.56554023
 -0.89520616]
Top 2 rows:
0       -0.200094
1       0.923716
```

```
dtype: float64
Last 2 rows:
2    -0.565540
3    -0.895206
dtype: float64
```

Q8: **Explain various statistical measures supported by pandas.**

Ans: **axes:** Print row index as well as column index.

sum: Calculates the sum of all series.

mean: Calculates mean of all series.

median: Calculates the median of all series.

std: Calculates standard deviation.

count: Calculates sum of various series.

cumsum: Calculates cumulative sum.

import pandas as pd

importnumpy as np

```
d = {'Name`:pd.Series(['Raja`, 'Raju`, 'Ricky`,
'Shiv`, 'Vishnu`, 'Ramesh`, 'Mahender`,
'Lious`, `Salman`, `SRK`, `VV`, `MM`]),
'Age`:pd.Series([25, 26, 25, 23, 30, 29, 23,
34, 40, 30,51, 46]),
'Rating`:pd.Series ([4.23, 3.24, 3.98, 2.56,
3.20, 4.6, 3.8, 3.78, 2.98, 4.80, 4.10, 3.65])}
df = pd.DataFrame(d)

print(df)

print('axes')

print(df.axes)

print('sum')

print('sum',df.sum())

print('sum of axis 1 ',df.sum(1))

print('mean',df.mean())

print('std',df.std())

print('count',df.count())

print('median',df.median())

print('cumsum',df.cumsum())
```

Calculates sum series wise/column wise

Calculates sum row wise

Output:

```
     Age    Name          Rating
0    25     Raja          4.23
1    26     Raju          3.24
2    25     Ricky         3.98
3    23     Shiv          2.56
4    30     Vishnu        3.20
5    29     Ramesh        4.60
6    23     Mahender      3.80
7    34     Lious         3.78
8    40     Salman        2.98
9    30     SRK           4.80
10   51     VV            4.10
11   46     MM            3.65
axes
[RangeIndex(start=0, stop=12, step=1),
Index(['Age`, 'Name`, 'Rating`],
dtype=`object`)]
sum
sum Age 382
Name
RajaRajuRickyShivVishnuRameshMahenderLiousSalm...
Rating 44.92
dtype: object
sum of axis 1 0 29.23
1     29.24
2     28.98
3     25.56
4     33.20
5     33.60
6     26.80
7     37.78
8     42.98
9     34.80
10    55.10
11    49.65
dtype: float64
mean Age 31.833333
Rating 3.743333
dtype: float64
```

```
std Age    9.232682
Rating     0.661628
dtype: float64
count Age  12
Name       12
Rating     12
dtype: int64
median Age 29.50
Rating      3.79
dtype: float64
cumsum  Age  Name  Rating
0    25  Raja  4.23
1    51  RajaRaju  7.47
2    76  RajaRajuRicky  11.45
3    99  RajaRajuRickyShiv  14.01
4   129  RajaRajuRickyShivVishnu  17.21
5   158  RajaRajuRickyShivVishnuRamesh  21.81
6   181  RajaRajuRickyShivVishnuRameshMahender  25.61
7   215  RajaRajuRickyShivVishnuRameshMahenderLious
29.39
8   255
RajaRajuRickyShivVishnuRameshMahenderLiousSalman
32.37
9   285
RajaRajuRickyShivVishnuRameshMahenderLiousSalm...
37.17
10  336
RajaRajuRickyShivVishnuRameshMahenderLiousSalm...
41.27
11  382
RajaRajuRickyShivVishnuRameshMahenderLiousSalm...
44.92
```

Most of the measures can be easily made available with the help of describe function.

```
import pandas as pd
import numpy as np
d = {'Name`:pd.Series (['Raja`, `Raju`,
`Ricky`, `Shiv`, `Vishnu`, `Ramesh`,
`Mahender`,
    'Lious`, `Salman`, `SRK`, `VV`, `MM`]),
    'Age`:pd.Series([25.00, 26, 25, 23, 30, 29,
    23, 34, 40, 30, 51, 46.00]),
```

```
          'Rating`:pd.Series ([4.2320, 3.274, 3.98,
          2.5628, 3.20,4.600, 3.800, 3.780, 2.980,
          4.8000, 4.1000,3.65])}
df = pd.DataFrame(d)
print (df.describe())
```

Output:

```
       ==============================
                 Age           Rating
       count    12.000000     12.000000
       mean     31.833333      3.746567
       std       9.232682      0.659021
       min      23.000000      2.562800
       25%      25.000000      3.255500
       50%      29.500000      3.790000
       75%      35.500000      4.133000
       max      51.000000      4.800000
```

Q9: Explain reindexing.

Ans: Reindexing allows us to modify the index of one data frame by keeping the other data frame as reference.

It can also be achieved by passing index and corresponding columns.

```
import pandas as pd
import numpy as np


d =
{'Name':pd.Series(['Raja','Raju','Ricky','Shiv','Vishnu','Ramesh','Mahender
',
  'Lious','Salman','SRK','VV','MM']),
  'Age':pd.Series([25,26,25,23,30,29,23,34,40,30,51,46]),

'Rating':pd.Series([4.23,3.24,3.98,2.56,3.20,4.6,3.8,3.78,2.98,4.80,4.10,3.
65])}
df = pd.DataFrame(d)
df_reindexed = df.reindex(index=[1,0,5], columns=['Age', 'Name', 'Rating'])
print(df_reindexed)
```

Retrieves following row index data from original data frame

Retrieves following columns from original data frame

Output:

```
    Age   Name    Rating
1   26    Raju    3.24
0   25    Raja    4.23
5   29    Ramesh  4.60
```

Q10: Explain bfill and ffill.

Ans: While reindexing NaN can be introduced .bfill and ffill are used to handle NaN.

```
import pandas as pd
import numpy as np
df1 = pd.DataFrame(np.random.randn(4,3),columns=['col1','col2','col3'])
df2 = pd.DataFrame(np.random.randn(2,3),columns=['col1','col2','col3'])
print(df2.reindex_like(df1))
```

Since df2 is re indexed to a higher value in rows it would causes NaN

Output:

```
       col1        col2       col3
0   -0.591340   -2.216463   0.305495
1    0.264238    0.406872  -0.879538
2    NaN         NaN        NaN
3    NaN         NaN        NaN
```

Bfill:

Fills the value from ahead value into the previous NaN value.

FFill:

Fills the value from behind value into the missing NaN value.

print(df2.reindex_like(df1,method='ffill'))

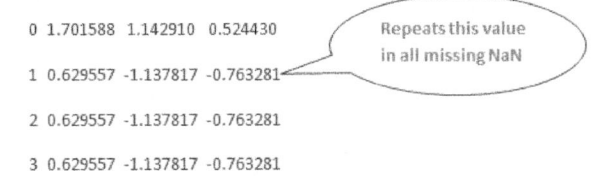

```
0  1.701588   1.142910   0.524430
1  0.629557  -1.137817  -0.763281
2  0.629557  -1.137817  -0.763281
3  0.629557  -1.137817  -0.763281
```

Repeats this value in all missing NaN

Q11: What all type of iterations are provided in pandas data frame?

Ans: **iteritems():** To iterate over the (key,value) pairs.

iterrows(): Iterate over the rows as (index,series) pairs.

itertuples(): Iterate over the rows as namedtuples.

Consider the following data frame sample:

```
     Age    Name       Rating
0    25     Raja       4.23
1    26     Raju       3.24
2    25     Ricky      3.98
3    23     Shiv       2.56
4    30     Vishnu     3.20
5    29     Ramesh     4.60
6    23     Mahender   3.80
7    34     Lious      3.78
8    40     Salman     2.98
9    30     SRK        4.80
10   51     VV         4.10
11   46     MM         3.65
```

forkey,value in df.iteritems():
print(key,value)
Output:

```
Age  0   25
     1   26
     2   25
     3   23
     4   30
     5   29
     6   23
     7   34
     8   40
     9   30
     10  51
     11  46
Name: Age, dtype: int64
Name 0 Raja
     1 Raju
     2 Ricky
     3 Shiv
     4 Vishnu
     5 Ramesh
     6 Mahender
     7 Lious
     8 Salman
     9 SRK
```

```
10  VV
11  MM
Name: Name, dtype: object
Rating 0  4.23
1  3.24
2  3.98
3  2.56
4  3.20
5  4.60
6  3.80
7  3.78
8  2.98
9  4.80
10  4.10
```
forrow_index,row in df.iterrows():
print (row_index,row)
```
0 Age 25
Name Raja
Rating 4.23
Name: 0, dtype: object
1 Age 26
Name Raju
Rating 3.24
Name: 1, dtype: object
2 Age 25
Name Ricky
Rating 3.98
Name: 2, dtype: object
3 Age 23
Name Shiv
Rating 2.56
Name: 3, dtype: object
4 Age 30
Name Vishnu
Rating 3.2
Name: 4, dtype: object
5 Age 29
Name Ramesh
Rating 4.6
```

```
Name: 5, dtype: object
6 Age 23
Name Mahender
Rating 3.8
Name: 6, dtype: object
7 Age 34
Name Lious
Rating 3.78
Name: 7, dtype: object
8 Age 40
Name Salman
Rating 2.98
Name: 8, dtype: object
9 Age 30
Name SRK
Rating 4.8
Name: 9, dtype: object
10 Age 51
Name VV
Rating 4.1
Name: 10, dtype: object
11 Age 46
Name MM
Rating 3.65
Name: 11, dtype: object
```

for row in df.itertuples():
print (row)
Output:
```
Pandas(Index=0, Age=25, Name=`Raja`, Rating=4.23)
Pandas(Index=1, Age=26, Name=`Raju`, Rating=3.24)
Pandas(Index=2, Age=25, Name=`Ricky`, Rating=3.98)
Pandas(Index=3, Age=23, Name=`Shiv`, Rating=2.56)
Pandas(Index=4, Age=30, Name=`Vishnu`, Rating=3.2)
Pandas(Index=5, Age=29, Name=`Ramesh`, Rating=4.6)
Pandas(Index=6, Age=23, Name=`Mahender`,
Rating=3.8)
Pandas(Index=7, Age=34, Name=`Lious`, Rating=3.78)
Pandas(Index=8, Age=40, Name=`Salman`,
Rating=2.98)
```

```
Pandas(Index=9,  Age=30, Name=`SRK`, Rating=4.8)
Pandas(Index=10, Age=51, Name=`VV`,  Rating=4.1)
Pandas(Index=11, Age=46, Name=`MM`,  Rating=3.65)
```

Q12: **Explain how sorting is supported in pandas?**

Ans: **sort_index:** Allows sorting on index(row) or column wise.

sort_values: Allows sorting on values.

Consider the following data frame:

```
     col2        col1
1    0.048787   -0.370136
4    0.846598   -0.475094
6    0.626231   -1.028268
2   -2.056041    0.280162
3   -1.398099   -0.425764
5    1.974402   -0.978264
9    1.511170   -0.589333
8   -1.744891   -0.919853
0   -1.273972    0.469276
7    1.794093    1.048517
```

sorted_df = unsorted_df.sort_values(by='col1')
print (sorted_df)

```
     col2      col1
6    0.626231 -1.028268
5    1.974402 -0.978264
8   -1.744891 -0.919853
9    1.511170 -0.589333
4    0.846598 -0.475094
3   -1.398099 -0.425764
1    0.048787 -0.370136
2   -2.056041  0.280162
0   -1.273972  0.469276
7    1.794093  1.048517
```

Results are sorted on col1 in ascending order

sorted_df=unsorted_df.sort_index(axis=1)

print (sorted_df)

```
   col1      col2
```
Columns are rearranged

```
1 -0.852017 -0.530043

4  0.422459  1.355061

6 -0.340375  0.226448

2  0.236609  0.074492

3  1.571648  0.770137

5  0.240715 -0.393545

9 -0.247026 -1.105864

8 -0.046523  0.003584

0 -1.024904 -0.761627

7  1.092764  2.268048
```

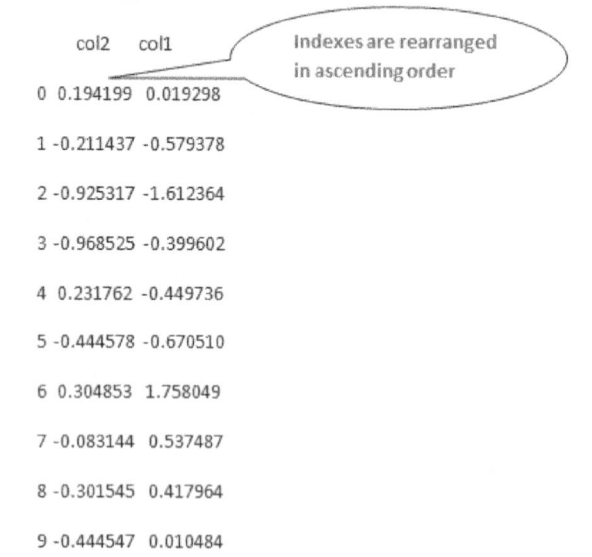

sorted_df=unsorted_df.sort_index()
print (sorted_df)

```
   col2      col1
```
Indexes are rearranged in ascending order

```
0  0.194199  0.019298

1 -0.211437 -0.579378

2 -0.925317 -1.612364

3 -0.968525 -0.399602

4  0.231762 -0.449736

5 -0.444578 -0.670510

6  0.304853  1.758049

7 -0.083144  0.537487

8 -0.301545  0.417964

9 -0.444547  0.010484
```

sorted_df=unsorted_df.sort_index(ascending=False)
print (sorted_df)

```
   col2       col1
9 -1.003009  -1.151731
```

```
8  1.317469  -0.774446
7 -0.170884   0.694429
6 -1.161735  -0.702071
5 -1.232564   0.843178
4 -0.550387   2.167216
3 -0.367910  -0.658615
2 -0.297523   0.277371
1  0.551069   1.218894
0  1.320420   0.439020
```

Q13: How to override default reload option in pandas?
Ans:

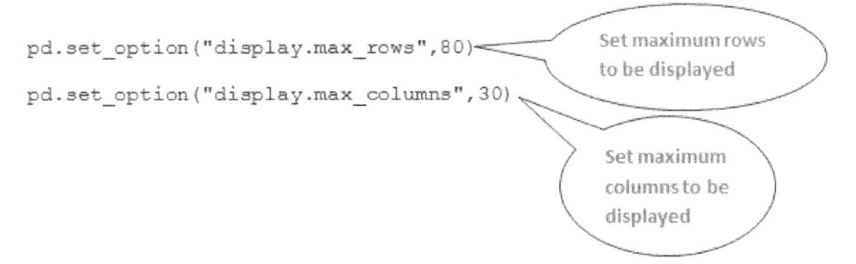

```
pd.set_option("display.max_rows",80)     ← Set maximum rows to be displayed
pd.set_option("display.max_columns",30)  ← Set maximum columns to be displayed
```

Q14: Explain various slicing options available with pandas?
Ans: Pandas supports the following slicing:

.loc() Label based
.iloc() Integer based
.ix() Both Label and Integer based

Consider the following data frame:

	A	B	C	D
a	-1.53558	0.297237	-0.56182	1.401168
b	0.473623	1.080733	0.095463	0.683253
c	-0.1642	0.823932	-0.66819	1.423232
d	0.943825	-0.40707	-0.04698	0.133415
e	-0.47114	-1.00112	-1.0575	0.843195
f	-0.35179	-1.47116	1.612342	-0.74294
g	-0.63809	0.231685	0.327186	-0.73119
h	-0.60686	-1.59435	-0.24473	-2.33809

```
print (df.loc[:,'A':'C'])   ← Performs slicing based on label of column only columns A to C would be fetched
```

	A	B	C
a	-1.53558	0.297237	-0.56182
b	0.473623	1.080733	0.095463
c	-0.1642	0.823932	-0.66819
d	0.943825	-0.40707	-0.04698
e	-0.47114	-1.00112	-1.0575
f	-0.35179	-1.47116	1.612342
g	-0.63809	0.231685	0.327186
h	-0.60686	-1.59435	-0.24473

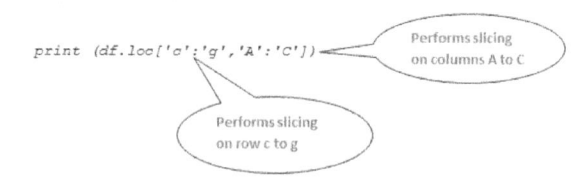

```
print (df.loc['c':'g','A':'C'])
```

Performs slicing on columns A to C

Performs slicing on row c to g

Output:

	A	B	C	D
c	-0.1642	0.823932	-0.66819	1.423232
d	0.943825	-0.40707	-0.04698	0.133415
e	-0.47114	-1.00112	-1.0575	0.843195
f	-0.35179	-1.47116	1.612342	-0.74294
g	-0.63809	0.231685	0.327186	-0.73119
h	-0.60686	-1.59435	-0.24473	-2.33809

```
print (df.iloc[1:5, 2:4])
```

Columns 2 to 4 would be fetched

Slices based on index number. Here row 1 to 5 would be fetched

	A	B	C	D
b	0.473623	1.080733	0.095463	0.683253
c	-0.1642	0.823932	-0.66819	1.423232
d	0.943825	-0.40707	-0.04698	0.133415
e	-0.47114	-1.00112	-1.0575	0.843195

`print (df.ix['c',:4])` ← Allows slicing on indexes as well as labels

	A	B	C	D
c	-0.1642	0.823932	-0.66819	1.423232

Q15: **Explain advanced statistics with pandas.**

Ans: Pandas support peak to peak, percentage change, covariance, and correlation on different series in data frame.

```
s1 = pd.Series(np.random.randn(10))

s2 = pd.Series(np.random.randn(10))

frame = pd.DataFrame({"s1":s1,"s2":s2})

print(frame)
print (frame.pct_change())   ← Calculates percentage change
print (frame.cov())          ← Calculates Covariance
print (frame.corr())         ← Calculates Correlation
```

Output

Data frame

```
          s1           s2
0   -1.448675    -1.045116
1    0.453446     0.558663
2   -0.577190     0.697816
3    0.085386    -0.181952
4    0.524836     0.379238
5    1.042358     1.001935
6    2.558341     0.182684
7    0.517772    -0.358159
8    0.442801    -0.475986
9    1.614731     1.121278
```

Pct change

```
          s1           s2
0        NaN         NaN
0   -1.448675    -1.045116
1   -1.313007    -1.534547
2   -2.272896     0.249081
3   -1.147933    -1.260745
```

```
4   5.146660   -3.084272
5   0.986064    1.641970
6   1.454378   -0.817669
7  -0.797614   -2.960538
8  -0.144794    0.328977
9   2.646625   -3.355698
```

Covariance:
```
         s1          s2
s1   1.211658    0.388197
s2   0.388197    0.484890
```

Correlation:
```
         s1          s2
s1   1.000000    0.506455
s2   0.506455    1.000000
```

Q16: **Explain rolling function.**

Ans: Rolling function allows us to define window size and perform various operations w.r.t. the window.

Expanding function is an alternative to rolling statistics is to use an expanding window, which yields the value of the statistic with all the data available up to that point in time.

Consider the following data frame:

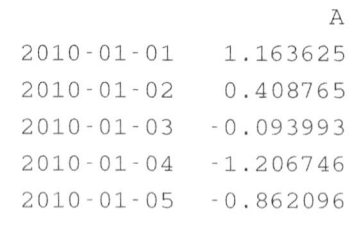

```
                    A
2010-01-01    1.163625
2010-01-02    0.408765
2010-01-03   -0.093993
2010-01-04   -1.206746
2010-01-05   -0.862096
```

Calculates rolling mean using the window size as 3

```
print(df.rolling(window=3).mean())
```

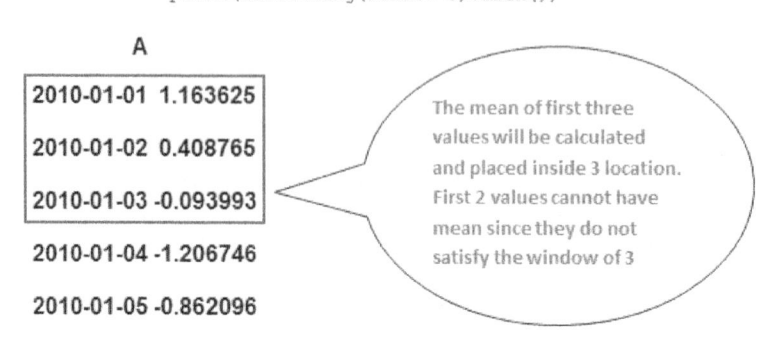

```
                 A
2010-01-01    1.163625
2010-01-02    0.408765
2010-01-03   -0.093993
2010-01-04   -1.206746
2010-01-05   -0.862096
```

The mean of first three values will be calculated and placed inside 3 location. First 2 values cannot have mean since they do not satisfy the window of 3

print (df.expanding(min_periods=3).mean())

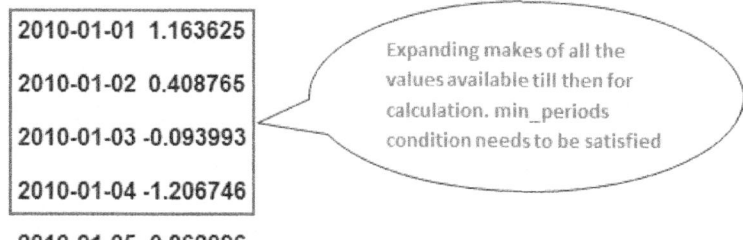

2010-01-01	1.163625
2010-01-02	0.408765
2010-01-03	-0.093993
2010-01-04	-1.206746

Expanding makes of all the values available till then for calculation. min_periods condition needs to be satisfied

2010-01-05 -0.862096

Q17: **How can we handle NA in pandas?**
Ans: We can handle NA in three ways:
   a. dropna: Removes the data where NA is present.
   b. pad
   c. backfill

Consider the following dataframe:

	one	Two	Three
a	0.121671	-0.90002	-0.11258
b	NaN	NaN	NaN
c	-1.15264	-0.70297	-0.76683
d	NaN	NaN	NaN
e	-0.03259	-0.75593	-0.3015
f	0.968174	0.107281	-1.42007
g	NaN	NaN	NaN
h	-0.06344	2.590979	-0.59222

dropna output
print (df.dropna())

	one	Two	three
a	0.121671	-0.90002	-0.11258
c	-1.15264	-0.70297	-0.76683
e	-0.03259	-0.75593	-0.3015
f	0.968174	0.107281	-1.42007
h	-0.06344	2.590979	-0.59222

Pad output

```
print (df.fillna(method='pad'))
```

	one	two	three
a	0.121671	-0.90002	0.11258
b	0.121671	-0.90002	0.11258
c	-1.15264	-0.70297	0.76683
d	-1.15264	-0.70297	0.76683
e	-0.03259	-0.75593	-0.3015
f	0.968174	0.107281	1.42007
g	0.968174	0.107281	1.42007
h	-0.06344	2.590979	0.59222

NaN are replaced by previous non NaN values

Backfill:

```
print (df.fillna(method='backfill'))
```

	one	two	three
a	0.121671	-0.90002	-0.11258
b	-1.15264	-0.70297	-0.76683
c	-1.15264	-0.70297	-0.76683
d	-0.03259	-0.75593	-0.3015
e	-0.03259	-0.75593	-0.3015
f	0.968174	0.107281	-1.42007
g	-0.06344	2.590979	-0.59222
h	-0.06344	2.590979	-0.59222

NaN is replaced with ahead values

Q18: **Explain group by function.**

Ans: **group_by** allows us to group data based on single or multiple columns.

It is equivalent to *Group by* clause supported in **Structured Query language (SQL)**.

Consider the following dataframe:

	Points	Rank	Team	Year
0	876	1	R	2014
1	789	2	R	2015
2	863	2	D	2014
3	673	3	D	2015
4	741	3	K	2014
5	812	4	K	2015
6	756	1	K	2016
7	788	1	K	2017
8	694	2	R	2016
9	701	4	RR	2014
10	804	1	RR	2015
11	690	2	R	2017

Will group the above data based on year

```
grouped = df.groupby('Year')
```

Year wise grouped

```
2014
   Points Rank Team Year
0    876    1    R  2014
2    863    2    D  2014
4    741    3    K  2014
9    701    4   RR  2014
2015
   Points  Rank  Team  Year
1     789     2     R  2015
3     673     3     D  2015
5     812     4     K  2015
10    804     1    RR  2015
2016
   Points  Rank  Team  Year
6     756     1     K  2016
8     694     2     R  2016
2017
   Points  Rank  Team  Year
7     788     1     K  2017
11    690     2     R  2017
```

Q19: Explain merge functions w.r.t data frame.

Ans: Data frame in pandas support merge operations in which two related data from diverse data frames can be brought in single view.

Consider the following left and right data frame:

Left

	FirstName	Id	subject_id
0	Vishwa	11	sub1
1	Mahesh	2	sub2
2	Kallu	33	sub4
3	Ballu	44	sub6
4	Mallu	55	sub5

Right

	LastName	Id	subject_id
0	Nara	11	sub1
1	Kal	2	sub4
2	Challu	3	sub3
3	Shana	4	sub6

Records matching by id on both the data frames would be returned

```
print ('id merge',pd.merge(left,right,on='id'))
```

Id	merge	FirstName	id2	subject_id_x	LastName	subject_id_y
	0	Vishwa	11	sub1	Nara	sub1
	1	Mahesh	2	sub2	Kal	sub4

Left merge:

In left merge, all data from left side will come and only those matching from right would come.

Left indicates everything from left

```
print ('left',pd.merge(left, right, on='id', how='left'))
```

NaN can be introduced

left	FirstName	id	subject_id_x	LastName	subject_id_y
0	Vishwa	11	sub1	Nara	sub1
1	Mahesh	2	sub2	Kal	sub4
2	Kallu	33	sub4	NaN	NaN
3	Ballu	44	sub6	NaN	NaN
4	Mallu	55	sub5	NaN	NaN

Right merge:

In right merge everything from right side comes and only matching in left would come else it would come as NaN.

print ('right',pd.merge(left, right, on='id', how='right'))

right	FirstName	Id	subject_id_x	LastName	subject_id_y
0	Vishwa	11	sub1	Nara	sub1
1	Mahesh	2	sub2	Kal	sub4
2	NaN	3	NaN	Challu	sub3
3	NaN	4	NaN	Shana	sub6

Outer merge:

Data from both left and right would come.

print ('outer',pd.merge(left, right, on='subject_id', how='outer'))

outer	FirstName	id_x	subject_id	LastName	id_y
0	Vishwa	11	sub1	Nara	11
1	Mahesh	2	sub2	NaN	NaN
2	Kallu	33	sub4	Kal	2
3	Ballu	44	sub6	Shana	4
4	Mallu	55	sub5	NaN	NaN
5	NaN	NaN	sub3	Challu	3

Q20: Explain concat method.

Ans: **Concat** method allows combining two different data frames either at row level or at column level.

Consider the following left and right data frame:

Left

	Name	Id	subject_id
1	Vishwa	11	sub1
2	Mahesh	2	sub2
3	Kallu	33	sub4
4	Ballu	44	sub6
5	Mallu	55	sub5

Right

	Name	Id	subject_id
1	Nara	11	sub1
2	Kal	2	sub4
3	Challu	3	sub3
4	Shana	4	sub6

print (pd.concat([left,right]))

	Name	Id	subject_id
0	Vishwa	11	sub1
1	Mahesh	2	sub2
2	Kallu	33	sub4
3	Ballu	44	sub6
4	Mallu	55	sub5
0	Nara	11	sub1
1	Kal	2	sub4
2	Challu	3	sub3
3	Shana	4	sub6

print (pd.concat([left,right],axis=1))

	Name	id	subject_id	Name	id	subject_id
0	Vishwa	11	sub1	Nara	11	sub1
1	Mahesh	2	sub2	Kal	2	sub4
2	Kallu	33	sub4	Challu	3	sub3
3	Ballu	44	sub6	Shana	4	sub6
4	Mallu	55	sub5	NaN	NaN	NaN

Q21: **Explain how time related range can be generated in pandas.**

Ans: Pandas support generating date range with the help of two functions **date_range** and **bdate_range** (business date range). Periods and frequency can be specified as attribute to the ranges.

start = pd.datetime(2018, 1, 1)
end = pd.datetime(2020, 1, 5)
print (pd.bdate_range(start, end))

Output:
```
DatetimeIndex(['2018-01-01', '2018-01-02',
'2018-01-03', '2018-01-04',
'2018-01-05', '2018-01-08', '2018-01-09',
'2018-01-10',
   '2018-01-11', '2018-01-12',
   ...
'2019-12-23', '2019-12-24', '2019-
   12-25', '2019-12-26',
```

```
'2019-12-27', '2019-12-30', '2019-12-31',
'2020-01-01',
    '2020-01-02', '2020-01-03'],
    dtype='datetime64[ns]', length=525, freq='B')
```

print (pd.date_range('1/1/2011', periods=5,freq='M'))

Output:

DatetimeIndex(['2011-01-31', '2011-02-28', '2011-03-31', '2011-04-30',

'2011-05-31'],

dtype='datetime64[ns]', freq='M')

Q22: Explain which all data sources can pandas retrieve values.

Ans: Pandas are capable of reading and writing from variety of sources.

Following are the sources and the corresponding read or write methods:

Format Type	Data Description	Reader	Writer
text	CSV	read_csv	to_csv
text	JSON	read_json	to_json
text	HTML	read_html	to_html
text	Local clipboard	read_clipboard	to_clipboard
binary	MS Excel	read_excel	to_excel
binary	HDF5 Format	read_hdf	to_hdf
binary	Feather Format	read_feather	to_feather
binary	Parquet Format	read_parquet	to_parquet
binary	Msgpack	read_msgpack	to_msgpack
binary	Stata	read_stata	to_stata
binary	SAS	read_sas	
binary	Python Pickle Format	read_pickle	to_pickle
SQL	SQL	read_sql	to_sql
SQL	Google Big Query	read_gbq	to_gbq
Remote data sources			

Format Type	Data Description	Reader	Writer
	Reads from remote data sources like • Google Finance • Morningstar • IEX • Robinhood • Enigma • Quandl • St.Louis FED (FRED) • Kenneth French's data library • World Bank • OECD • Eurostat • Thrift Savings Plan • Nasdaq Trader symbol definitions • Stooq • MOEX	web.DataReader	

Q23: Can you compare some of the functions of R and Python?

Ans: **Filtering, sampling, and Querying**

R	Pandas
dim(dataframe)	dataframe.shape
head(dataframe)	dataframe.head()
slice(dataframe, 1:100)	dataframe.iloc[:99]
filter(dataframe, column1 == 1, column2 == 1)	dataframe.query('column1 == 1 & column2 == 1')
dataframe[dataframe$column1 == 1 & dataframe$column2 == 1,]	dataframe[(dataframe.column1 == 1) & (dataframe.column2 == 1)]
select(dataframe, column1, column2)	dataframe[['column1', 'column2']]
select(dataframe, column1:column3)	dataframe.loc[:, 'column1':'column3']

R	Pandas
select(dataframe, -(column1:column3))	dataframe.drop(cols_to_drop, axis=1) but see [1]
distinct(select(dataframe, column1))	dataframe[['column1']].drop_duplicates()
distinct(select(dataframe, column1, column2))	dataframe[['column1', 'column2']].drop_duplicates()
sample_n(dataframe, 10)	dataframe.sample(n=10)
sample_frac(dataframe, 0.01)	dataframe.sample(frac=0.01)

Sorting

R	Pandas
arrange(dataframe, column1, column2)	dataframe.sort_values(['column1', 'column2'])
arrange(dataframe, desc(column1))	dataframe.sort_values('column1', ascending=False)

Transforming

R	Pandas
select(dataframe, col_one = column1)	dataframe.rename(columns={'column1': 'col_one'})['col_one']
rename(dataframe, col_one = column1)	dataframe.rename(columns={'column1': 'col_one'})
mutate(dataframe, c=a-b)	dataframe.assign(c=dataframe.a-dataframe.b)

Aggregate/Grouping functions

R	Pandas
summary(dataframe)	dataframe.describe()
gdataframe <- group_by(dataframe, column1)	gdataframe = dataframe.groupby('column1')
summarise(gdataframe, avg=mean(column1, na.rm=TRUE))	dataframe.groupby('column1').agg({'column1': 'mean'})
summarise(gdataframe, total=sum(column1))	dataframe.groupby('column1').sum()

Q24: How to print a histogram using pandas?

Ans: Using **series.value_counts()** functions we can easily generate the value and its corresponding count.

import pandas as pd

importnumpy as np
s = pd.Series([1,1,100,120,30,40,60,60])
print(s)
print(s.value_counts())
Output:

```
s
0    1
1    1
2    100
3    120
4    30
5    40
6    60
7    60
```

Histogram

Value count

```
60    2
1     2
30    1
40    1
100   1
120   1
```

CHAPTER 5
Scipy and its Applications

Note: [Q: Question Number and Ans: Answer]

Q1: Explain Scipy library.

Ans: Scipy is used for scientific computation. It is a collection of components and provides eco system for scientific computing.

Data and computation:
- pandas, provides ease of use and very high performing data
- SymPy, for symbolic mathematics and computer algebra.
- scikit-image used for image processing.
- scikit-learn is used for machine learning.
- h5py and PyTables can both access data stored in the HDF5 format.

Q2: Explain how can we perform Normality Tests.

Ans: Normality tests are the ones which test for data distribution in the form of Gaussian.

Each of this has following assumptions on input and output:

Input assumptions:
- Observations in each sample are independent and identically distributed.

Output assumptions:
- H0: the sample has a Gaussian distribution
- H1: the sample does not have a Gaussian distribution

There are three types of test within.

All the three types are supported as a part of scipy.

```
import scipy.stats as ss
Shapiro-Wilk Test
stat, p = ss.shapiro(data)
D`Agostino`s K^2 Test
stat, p = ss.normaltest(data)
Anderson-Darling Test
result =ss.anderson(data)
```

Conclusion: If calculate p value < alpha, we can conclude null hypothesis rejected else it cannot be rejected.

Q3: Explain how can we perform correlation test?

Ans: **Pearson's Correlation Coefficient**

Tests have a linear relationship that exist between two data set.

Input Assumptions:

All these are made w.r.t Observations
- They are independent and identically distributed
- They are normally distributed
- They have the same variance

Output assumptions:
- H0: the two samples are independent.
- H1: two samples have dependancy.
```
import scipy.stats
corr, p = scipy.stats.pearsonr(data1, data2)
```

Based on value of corr and p we can conclude whether their relationship between both columns.

Spearman's Rank Correlation and Kendall's Rank Correlation. Both of them have same input and output assumptions.

Tests whether monotonic relationship exists between data set.

Input assumptions:

All assumptions are made w.r.t. observations:
- They are independent and identically distributed
- They can be ranked

Output assumptions:
- H0: The two samples are independent
- H1: There is a dependency between the samples

Spearman's Rank Correlation
```
import scipy.stats
corr, p = scipy.stats
 .spearmanr(data1, data2)
```

Kendall's Rank Correlation
```
import scipy.stats
corr, p = scipy.stats .kendalltau(data1, data2)
```

Based on value of corr and p we can conclude whether their relationship between both columns.

Chi-Squared Test

Tests independence between two categorical variables:

Input assumptions:
- Observations are independent.
- 25 or more examples in each cell are required w.r.t. the contingency table.

Output assumptions:
- H0: the two samples are independent.
- H1: there is a dependency between the samples.
```
import scipy.stats
stat, p, dof, expected = scipy.stats .chi2_contingency(table)
```

Q4: Explain tests pertaining to Parametric Statistical Hypothesis Tests.

Ans: Comparison of data is done by the following test:

Student's t-test

It tests whether the means of two independent samples are significantly different.

Input assumptions:

All assumptions are made w.r.t observation.
- They are independent and identically distributed (iid).

- They are normally distributed.
- They have the same variance.

Output assumptions:
- H0: the means of the samples are equal
- H1: the means of the sam ples are unequal
  ```
  import scipy.stats as ss
  stat, p = ss.ttest_ind(data1, data2)
  ```

Paired Student's t-test

Tests whether the significant difference exists between the means of two paired samples.

Input assumptions:
- Observations in each sample are independent and identically distributed
- Observations in each sample are normally distributed
- Observations in each sample have the same variance
- Observations across each sample are paired

Output assumptions:
- H0: the means of the samples are equal
- H1: the means of the samples are unequal
  ```
  import scipy.stats
  stat, p = scipy.stats.ttest_rel(data1, data2)
  ```

Analysis of Variance Test (ANOVA)

It tests whether the means of two or more independent samples are significantly different.

Input assumptions:

All assumptions are made w.r.t observation:
- They are independent and identically distributed (iid).
- They are normally distributed.
- They have the same variance.

Output assumptions:
- H0: the means of the samples are equal.
- H1: one or more of the means of the samples are unequal.
  ```
  import scipy.stats
  stat, p = scipy.stats.f_oneway(data1, data2,
  ...)
  ```

Q5: Explain how to test Nonparametric Statistical Hypothesis Tests.

Ans: Mann-Whitney U Test:

It tests whether the two independent samples are equal or not.

Input Assumptions:

All assumptions are made w.r.t observation:
- They are independent and identically distributed.
- They can be ranked.

Output Assumptions:
- H0: the distributions of both samples are equal.
- H1: the distributions of both samples are not equal.

```
import scipy.stats
stat, p = scipy.stats.mannwhitneyu(data1, data2)
```

Q6: Implement logistic regression in Python?

Ans: sklearn.linear_model contains LogisticRegression which can be used to represent logistic regression.

```
import sklearn.linear_model as sklm
logmodel = sklm.LogisticRegression()
logmodel.fit(feautures,label)
y_pred= logmodel.predict(X_test)
```

- `logmodel.fit(...)` — Make the model with the help of train data. features and label represents data and corresponding labels used for training the model
- `y_pred= logmodel.predict(X_test)` — Predict using the above created and enhanced model with test data

Q7: Explain how to implement decision tree in Python.

Ans: sklearn.tree module contains DecisionTreeClassifier which can be used for classification.

```
import sklearn.tree as slt
model = slt.DecisionTreeClassifier()
model.fit(feautures,label)
y_pred = model.predict(X_test)
```

Fit the model using features and label where features represents data and labels represents labels generated used for training

Q8: How to implement Random forest in Python?

Ans: **sklearn.ensemble** module contains RandomForestClassifier which can be used for Random forest generation.

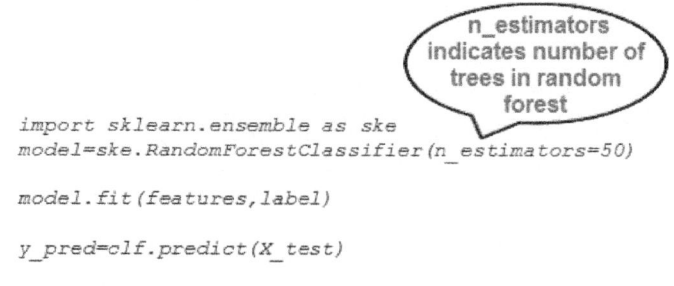

(n_estimators indicates number of trees in random forest)

```
import sklearn.ensemble as ske
model=ske.RandomForestClassifier(n_estimators=50)

model.fit(features,label)

y_pred=clf.predict(X_test)
```

For regression type we will use **RandomForestRegressor** instead of **RandomForestClassifier**.

Q9: How to implement support vector machine in Python?

Ans: **sklearn.svm** module contains SVC which is used for svm.

SVM for linear model code:

(Indicates linearly separable approach)

```
import sklearn.svm as svm
model = svm.SVC(kernel='linear')
model.fit(feautures,label)
y_pred=clf.predict(X_test)
```

SVM for non-linear/polynomial mode code

(The value of kernel to poly and degree indicates that this svm supports polynomial approach)

```
import sklearn.svm as svm
model = svm.SVC(kernel='poly', degree=9)
model.fit(features, label)
y_pred=clf.predict(X_test)
```

Q10: Which all kernels are supported by svm in Python?

Ans: Linear, poly, sigmoid (which returns 0 or 1 kernel='sigmoid') and gaussian (to support gaussian distribution kernel=rbf)

Q11: Implement KNN algorithm using Python.

Ans: **sklearn.neighbors** module contains **KNeighborsClassifier** which can be used for classification:

```
import sklearn.neighbors as sn
model = sn.KNeighborsClassifier(n_neighbors=3)
model.fit(features,label)
predicted= model.predict(X_test)
```

n_neighbors stands for number of neighbors used for classification

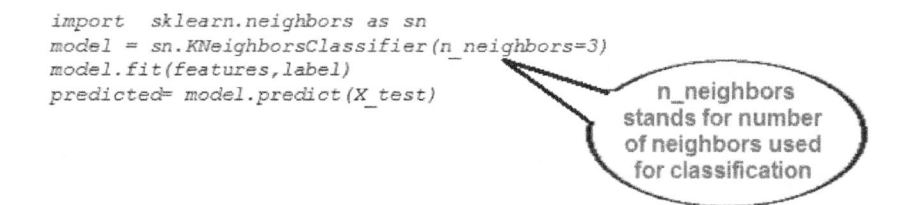

Q12: How to select k in KNN algorithm?

Ans: Finding an optimal value of **k** is very important in order to ensure success of KNN algorithm.

The value of **k** is heavily dependent on the data set.

A very small value of **k** implies noise can have a bigger influence on the result.

A large value of **k** implies more calculations which can be time and memory consuming.

Mostly Odd classes are preferred and **k= sqrt(noOfElements)** is generally taken as an approach to find **k**.

Alternatively, Elbow method can also be used. In the case of Elbow method. In Elbow method we calculate the sum of squared errors (SSE) for different values of k and plot the same.

The one which looks like an elbow is selected as the optimal.

Q13: How to implement K means in Python?

Ans: We can implement K means with the help of **sklearn.cluster** module which contains KMeans.

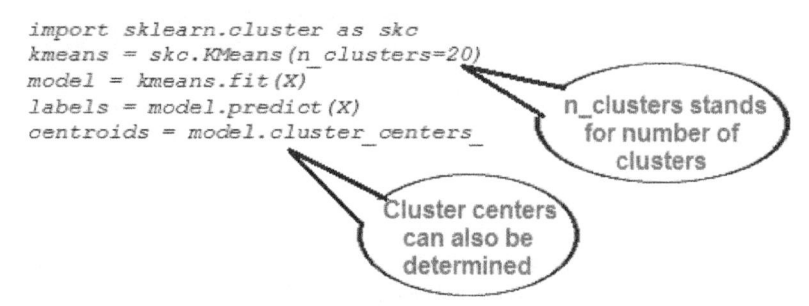

```
import sklearn.cluster as skc
kmeans = skc.KMeans(n_clusters=20)
model = kmeans.fit(X)
labels = model.predict(X)
centroids = model.cluster_centers_
```

n_clusters stands for number of clusters

Cluster centers can also be determined

Q14: How can accuracy of any model be calculated?

Ans: Following approaches can be used to determine accuracy:

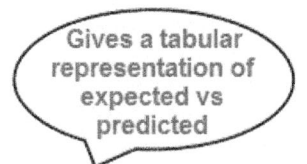

1.
   > Gives a tabular representation of expected vs predicted

   ```
   import sklearn.metrics as skm
   skm.confusion_matrix(labels_train, pred)
   ```

2.
   ```
   from sklearn.metrics import accuracy_score
   accuracy_score(labels_test,pred)
   ```

   > Accuracy score is a good indicator of how the algorithm has performed

3.
   ```
   from sklearn.metrics import classification_report
   report = classification_report(Y_test, predicted)
   ```

   > displays the precision, recall, f1-score and support for each class

4.
   ```
   from sklearn.metrics import recall_score
   recall_score(label,predicted)
   ```

   > Recall /sensitivity is the fraction of positives events predicted correctly

5.
   ```
   from sklearn.metrics import precision_score
   precision_score(label,predicted)
   ```

   > is the fraction of predicted positives events that are actually positive

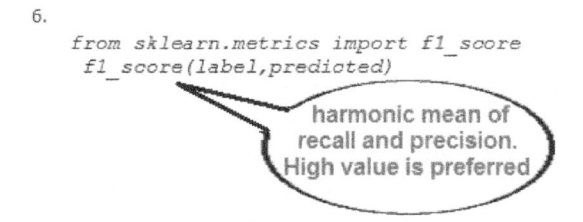

6.
```
from sklearn.metrics import f1_score
f1_score(label,predicted)
```
(harmonic mean of recall and precision. High value is preferred)

Q15: Explain regression metrics.

Ans: Regression metrics gives an indication of how the regression algorithm performed.

Following are the important ones:

Metric name	Definition	Code in Python
Mean Absolute Error (MAE)	Sum of the absolute differences between predictions and actual values.	*import sklearn as sk* *result =sk.model_selection.cross_val_score(model, X, Y, scoring='**neg_mean_absolute_error**')* *print(results.mean(), results.std())*
Root Mean Squared Error (RMSE)	It is the standard deviation of the prediction errors.	from sklearn.metrics import mean_squared_error from math import sqrt rmse = sqrt(mean_squared_error(y_actual, y_predicted))

Q16: Explain how we can print a decision tree or see the rules of the decision tree?

Ans: export_text can help us in achieving the above objective.

By passing the created model to the above function, we can get the rules printed out

```
fromsklearn.tree.export import export_text
dcrules = export_text(model, feature_names=list(train))
print(dcrules)
```

In the below example,dcrules is the extracted rule after passing the created model to export function:

```
|---Age<=0.80
| |---Salary<=0.65
| | |---Age<=-0.19
| | | |---class:0
```

```
|||---Age>-0.19
||||---Salary<=-0.06
|||||---class:0
||||---Salary>-0.06
|||||---Salary<=0.40
||||||---Salary<=0.03
|||||||---class:1
```

Q17: What is the use of boosting techniques?

Ans: Boosting techniques fall under the family of ensemble algorithms. In boosting techniques, a collection of many classifiersthatcan be weak in nature can be combined together to form a new classifier thatcan be strong.

It can be said that in boosting, a series of various classifiers are made progressively in which each classifier tries to solve the reduced the error of earlier one. The end product after this would be a refined classifier with better performance as compared to earlier

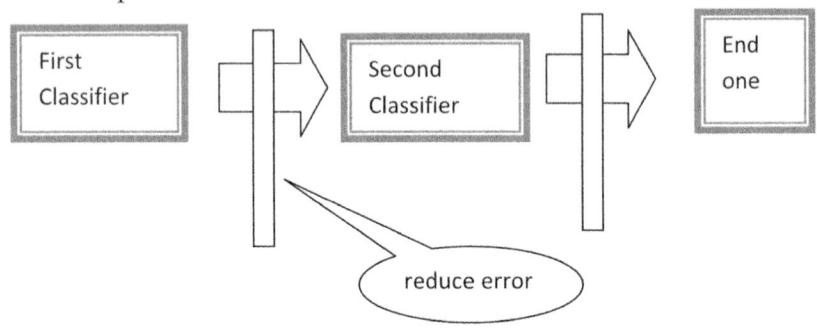

```
┌──────────┐      ┌──────────┐      ┌──────┐
│  First   │ ──▶  │  Second  │ ──▶  │ End  │
│Classifier│      │Classifier│      │ one  │
└──────────┘      └──────────┘      └──────┘
                       │
                  reduce error
```

Q18: Explain some of the advantages and disadvantages of boosting techniques?

Ans: **Advantages**
- Since they are ensemble model, the predictions are easy to interpret.
- Predictions are better are compared to normal classifiers.
- Over fitting can be handled to a good extent with the help of this technique.

Disadvantages:
- Outliers are important to consider. If not handled properly they can affect the entire model.
- Other than XGBBoost, most other algorithms are sequential thus limiting the scope of running it in parallel.

Q19: What is AdaBoost?

Ans: ADA, also known asthe Adaptive Boosting technique, was found by Yoav Freund and Robert Schapire. Since it is a boosting technique, the aim of this would be to find a new strong classifier from the collection of various weak classifiers.

It findsa major application with a decision tree or binary classification.

Generally,the ADA boost makes use of decision stumps, which are decision trees of one level.

The instance in the training data set is weighted. This is very important and distinct as compared to majority voting as the importance of each output is taken as per weightage.

Thus the process is to make use of decision stump to take input variable and predict binary values as classification.

By using the above misclassification rate is calculated.

Using the weighted sum,the stage value is then calculated.

Using this, training weights are updated,which gives more weightage to wrongly predicted instances and less weightage to properly predicted instances.

Weak models thatare added in the sequence are then trained using the weighted training data.

The above process is repeated until the desired accuracy is achieved, or no more improvements are possible.

Shown below is the code for Ada boosting

```
fromsklearn.ensemble import AdaBoostClassifier
booster = AdaBoostClassifier()
n_estimators = 50 (default value)
base_estimator = DecisionTreeClassifier (default value)
booster.fit(x_train,y_train)
booster.predict(x_test)
```

Q20: Explain Gradient boosting?

Ans: Gradient boosting makes use of the trained sequence model. It makes use of Gradient descent function, which calculates the local minimum of a given function. Thus we try to find the local minimum function for loss.

The procedure is to construct new learners whoare also known as the base and which can be correlated with negative gradient descent of the loss function,

```
fromsklearn.ensemble import
GradientBoostingClassifier #For Classification
#from sklearn.ensemble import
GradientBoostingRegressor #For Regression
classifier = GradientBoostingClassifier(n_
estimators, learning_rate, max_depth)
classifier.fit(X_train, y_train)
```

n_estimators: indicatesthe number of weak learners

learning_rate: determines the contribution of weak learners in the final combination

max_depth: maximum depth of the individual regression estimators. This limits the number of nodes in the tree.

Q21: Explain XGBoost?

Ans: TheXGBoost,also known as eXtreme Gradient Boostingis a set of algorithms /library for developing fast and high-performance gradient boosting tree models.

It makes use of gradient boosting framework

Some of the features are:

- Automatic handling of missing data values.
- Parallelization of tree construction is possible
- Makes use of the second partial derivatives of the loss function. This is the major difference as compared to other gradient algorithms. While other algorithms makes use of loss function which is first order derivative , XGB makes use of second order derivative which also gives the direction of the gradient
- Advanced regularization techniques are used.

Sample snippet

```
import pandas as pd
fromxgboost import XGBClassifier
fromsklearn.metrics import accuracy_score

model = XGBClassifier()
model.fit(x,y)
predict_train = model.predict(test_x)
accuracy_train = accuracy_
score(train_y,predict_train)
```

Q22: Explain the differences/similarities between bagging and Boosting?

Ans: **Similarities:**
- Both belong to the method of algorithms which are known as ensemble i.e. which generates gets 1 learner from N classifiers
- Both work by dividing the original dataset into smaller units
- Average of outputs are taken into consideration
- Both try to increase performance

Following table shows the differences:

Bagging	Boosting
New models from previous models are not made	New models are made based upon failure from previous models
Weights are not assigned to the training set	Weights are assigned to the training set
Equally weighted average is used	More weight is given to one which isdifficult and vice versa
Bagging solves over fitting	Boosting solves bias problem

Q23: Write a small snippet to perform operation with neural networks using tensorflow and keras?

Ans:
```
import numpy as np
import keras.models as km
import keras.layers as kl
```
Loading the data from a file and dividing the data into input and output

```
data = np.loadtxt('input.csv`, delimiter=`,`)
ip = data[:,0:100]
op = data[:,100]
```

Building the model with three layer shown

```
model = km.Sequential()
model.add(kl.Dense(200, input_dim=100, activation=`relu`))
model.add(kl.Dense(100, activation=`relu`))
model.add(kl.Dense(1, activation=`sigmoid`))
model.compile(loss=`binary_crossentropy`, optimizer=`adam`, metrics=['accuracy`])
model.fit(ip, op, epochs=200, batch_size=40)
```

Evaluation of model

```
accuracy = model.evaluate(ip, op)
print('Accuracy: %.5f` % (accuracy*100))
```

CHAPTER 6
Matplotlib Samples to Remember

Note: [Q: Question Number and Ans: Answer]

Q1: Explain how to draw bar plot.

Ans:
```
from matplotlib import pyplot as plt

a1= [5,8,10]

b1= [12,16,6]

a2 = [6,9,11]

b2 = [6,15,7]

plt.bar(a1, b1, align = 'center')

plt.bar(a2, b2, color = 'g', align = 'center')

plt.title('Bar graph sample')

plt.ylabel('Y axis')

plt.xlabel('X axis')

plt.show()
```

(Generates bar using a2 and b2)

(Name given to x and y co-ordinate in graph)

(Display plot generated)

Bar Graph Sample

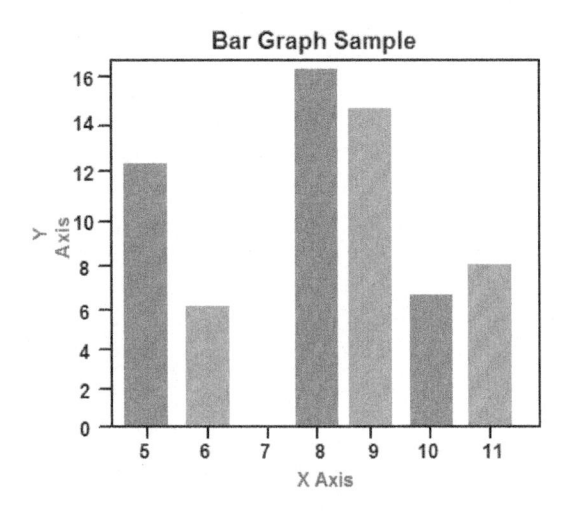

Q2: How to draw histogram?
Ans:

```
from matplotlib import pyplot as plt

import numpy as np


data = np.array([22,87,5,43,56,73,55,54,11,20,51,5,79,31,27])

plt.hist(data, bins = [0,20,40,60,80,100])

plt.title("Histogram of age")

plt.show()
```

Histogram generated using data and groups represented by bins

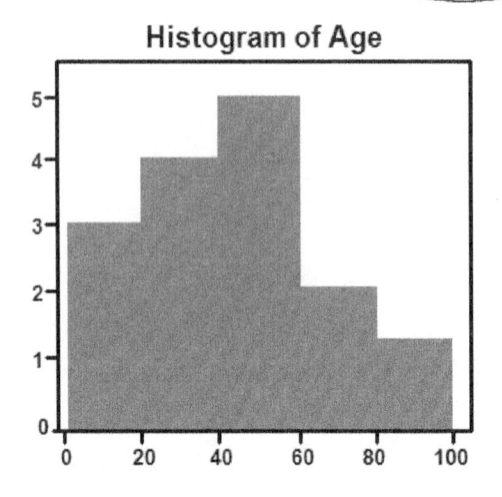

Histogram of Age

Q3: How to draw line chart?

Ans: **importnumpy as np**
frommatplotlib import pyplot as plt
frommatplotlib.backends.backend_pdf import PdfPages

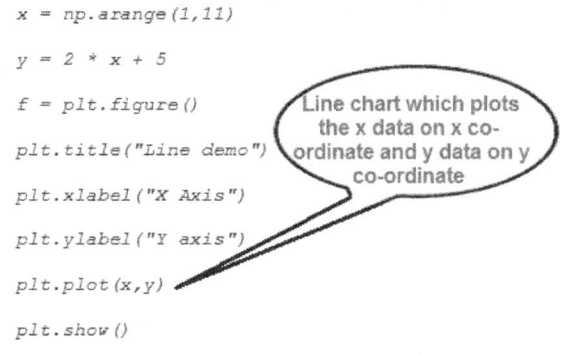

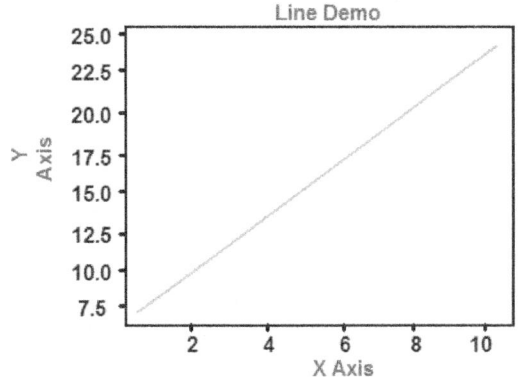

```
x = np.arange(1,11)
y = 2 * x + 5
f = plt.figure()
plt.title("Line demo")
plt.xlabel("X Axis")
plt.ylabel("Y axis")
plt.plot(x,y)
plt.show()
```

Line chart which plots the x data on x co-ordinate and y data on y co-ordinate

Line Demo

Q4: Draw Pie chart.

Ans:
```
import matplotlib.pyplot as plt

labels = ['Milk', 'Ice cream', 'Cold Drink', 'Lassi']
sizes = [48.4, 30.6, 20, 11]
colors = ['yellowgreen', 'lightskyblue', 'lightcoral','gold']
patches, texts = plt.pie(sizes, colors=colors, shadow=True, startangle=90)
plt.legend(patches, labels, loc="best")
plt.axis('equal')
plt.tight_layout()
plt.show()
```

Data passed as sizes with colors and extra attributes

Legend created with labels

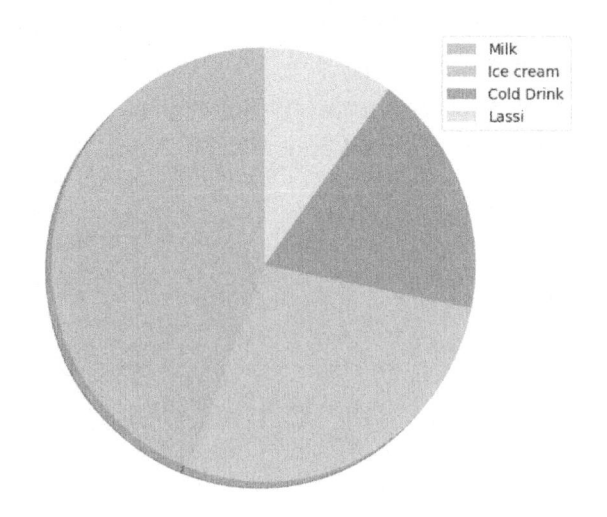

Q5: How to get the equation of the line printed line plot?

Ans: Using following snippet of code same can be achieved

```
plt.title('$y= slope * x+ intercept))
```

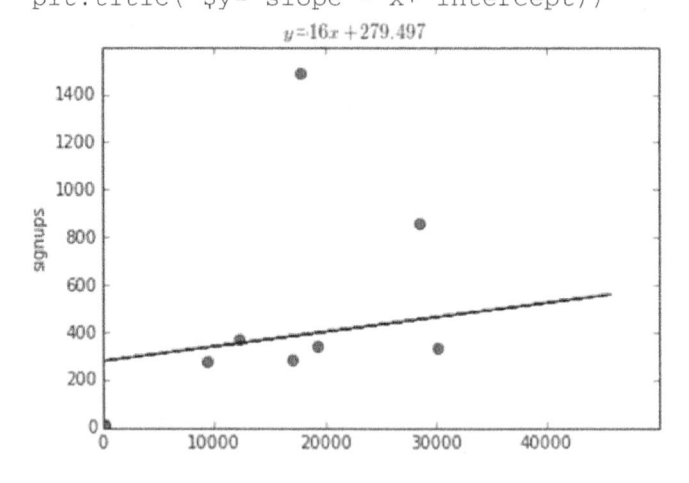

$y = 16x + 279.497$

Q6: Draw scatter plot.

Ans:

```
import numpy as np
import matplotlib.pyplot as plt

N = 100
x = np.random.rand(N)
y = np.random.rand(N)
colors = (0,100,100)
area = np.pi*4

plt.scatter(x, y, s=area, c=colors, alpha=0.5)
plt.title('Scatter plot sample')
plt.xlabel('X')
plt.ylabel('Y')
plt.show()
```

Scatter plot created with sample generated data

CHAPTER 7
Statistics with Excel Sheet

Note: [Q: Question Number and Ans: Answer]

Q1: Does Excel has any support for statistics?

Ans: Yes, Excel sheet do provide a lot of support for statistics with few add-ins like *Analysis Tool pack*. In order to enable this analysis tool pack, select excel options and the go to Add-ins option and enable *AnalysisToolPak*.

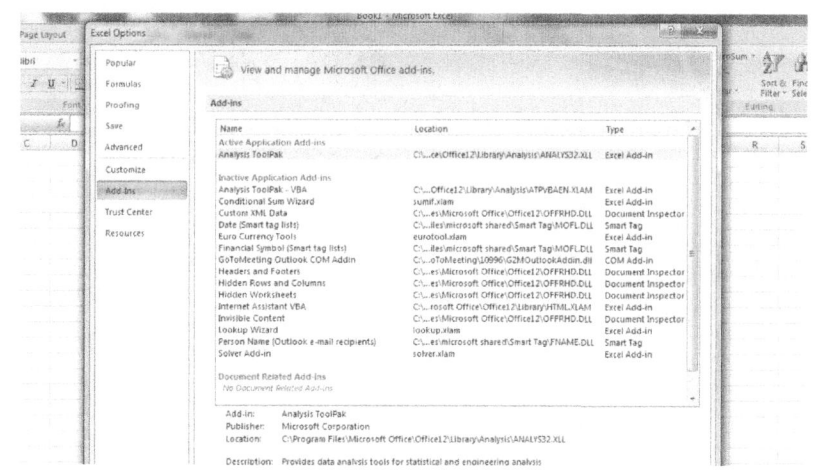

Once done, the data analysis option is enabled in Data tab of excel, it can be seen under the **Data** tab as shown in the image down below:

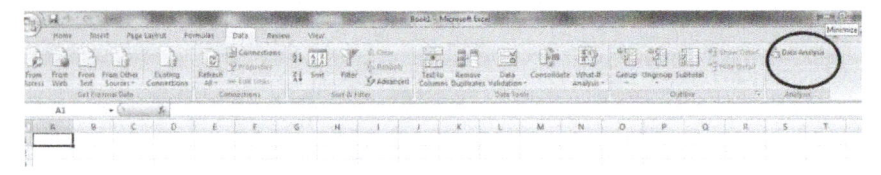

Q2: Find correlation using Excel.

Ans: Correlation can be easily found with the help of **CORREL** function of Analysis Toolpak.

Select **Data Analysis** → Select **correlation** as an option.

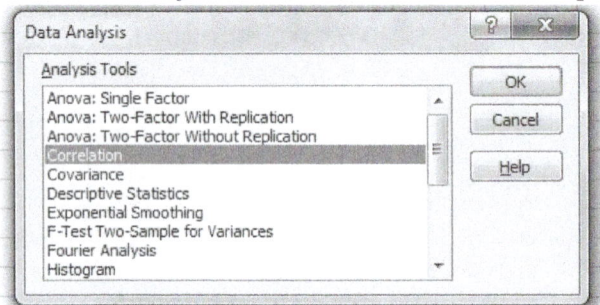

After selecting **Correlation** from Data Analysis select the corresponding input field and set output values to be displayed on the excel sheet by setting **Output Range** available under **Output options**,

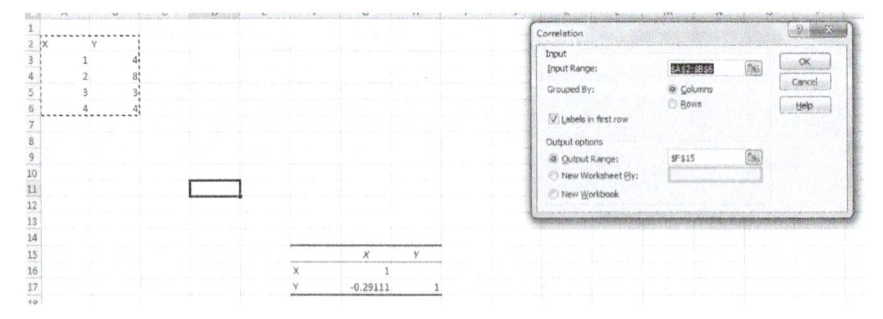

and after **OK** is clicked, the result for same of Covariance can be found on excel sheet.

Q3: How to get Histogram in excel?

Ans: To get Histogram in excel we generally require values and corresponding bins. Bins represent the range in which frequency is calculated.

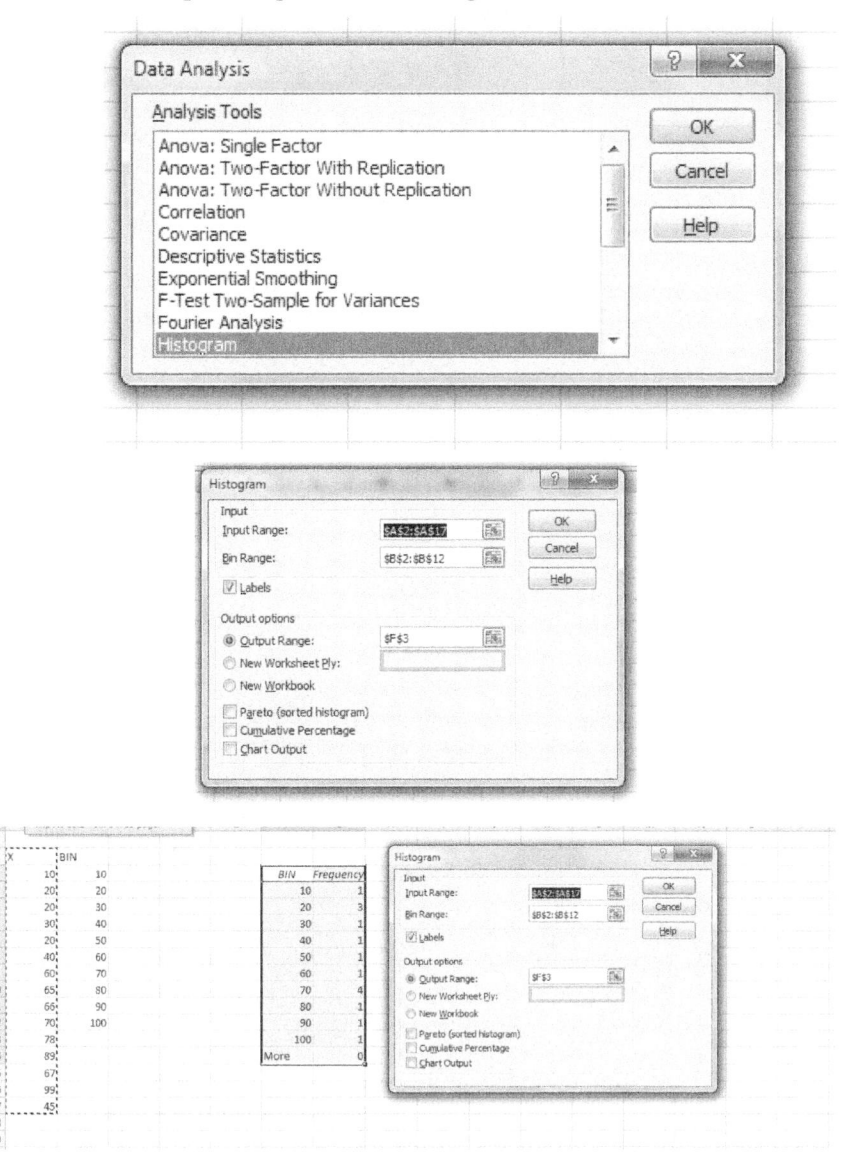

From **Data Analysis** → select **Histogram** function → we can select input range and bins range

Q4: **Explain how to get Descriptive Statistics using Excel.**

Ans: To get **Descriptive Statistics** select **Data Analysis** ⇒ Select **Descriptive Analysis** ⇒ then select different statistics you prefer.

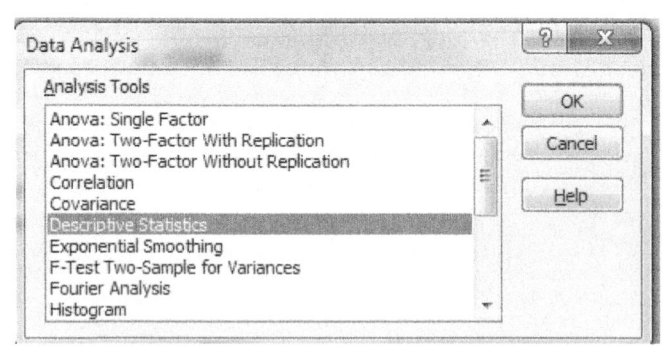

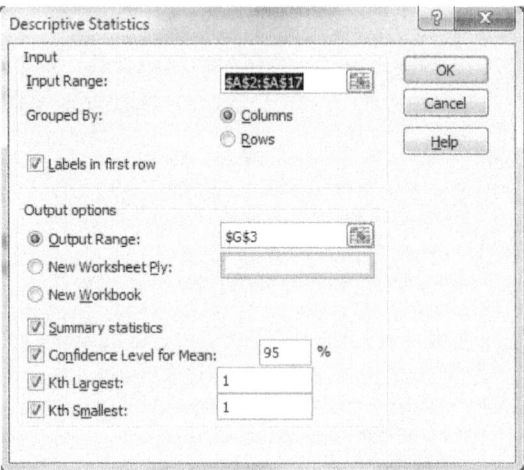

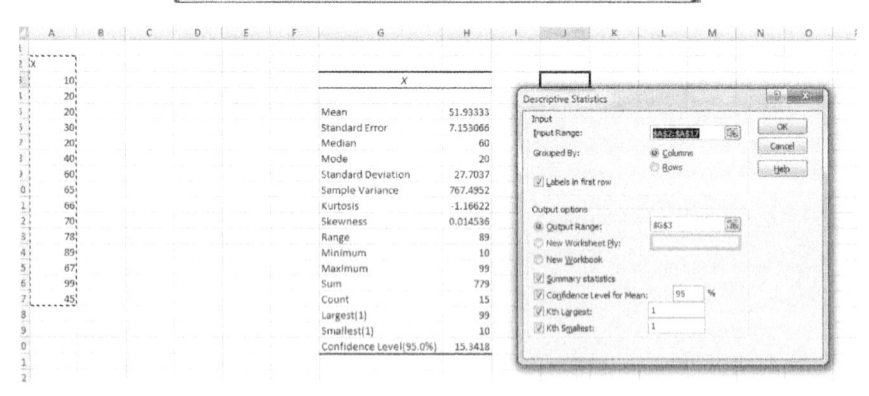

Q5: Explain how to perform Anova in excel?

Ans: To perform **Anova** select **Data Analysis** ⇒ **Anova: Single factor**

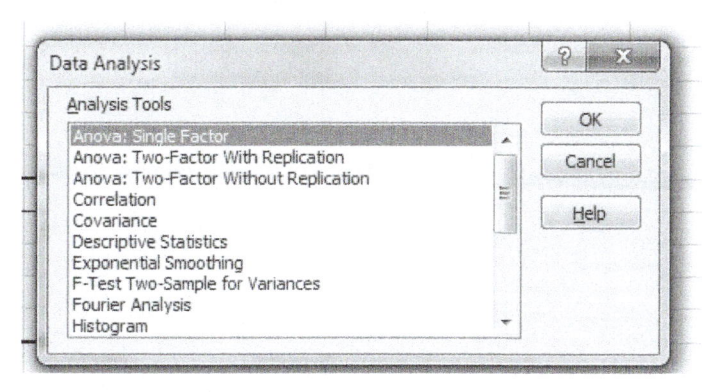

Select corresponding input and output values.

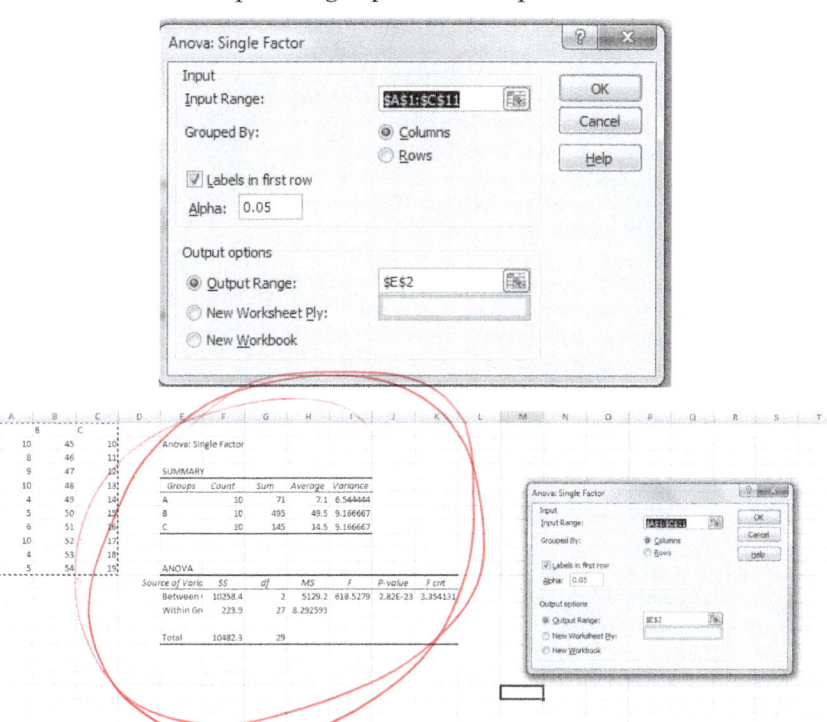

Based upon the value of F and F critical, we can conclude whether null hypothesis is rejected or accepted.

Q6: Explain how to perform Rank and Percentile in excel.

Ans: From **Data Analysis** → select **Rank and Percentile**

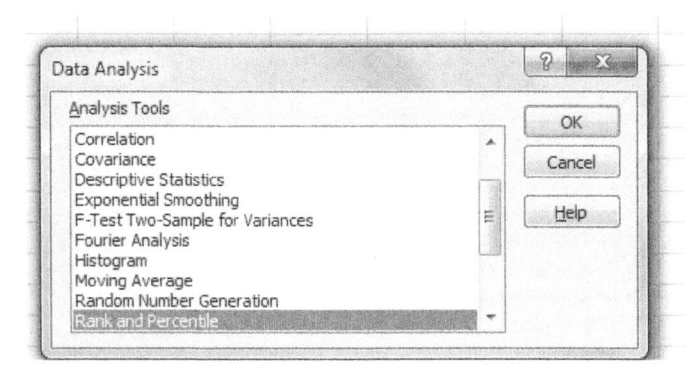

Select the input and output range to get the answer:

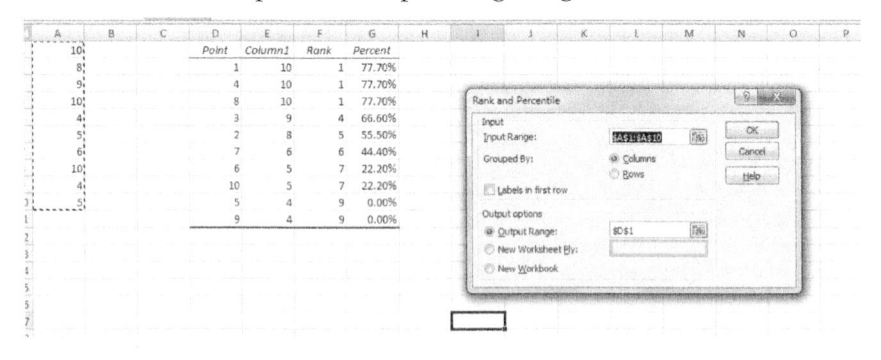

Printed by Amazon Italia Logistica S.r.l.
Torrazza Piemonte (TO), Italy